"An intelligent, sensitive quest into the soul of
one woman mirrors the searching hearts of us all.
LOOK UP! is a beautiful book of solitude and
inquiry into painful longings, but also into the
glory of our lives."

— Dale Carlson, owner, Bick Publishing House,
and author of more than 60 books

::

"As eloquent as it is enlivening, *LOOK UP!* evokes
more than an understanding of the vast and wonderful
lessons to be gleaned in the natural world. Filled with
grounded yet soaring flights of reflection and yearning
for balance in a frenetic world, it is a walk in the woods
of life—a tonic for both mind and soul."

— Mary O'Connor, award-winning poet
and author of *Life Is Full of Sweet Spots*

LOOK UP!
Musings on the Nature of Mindfulness

∷

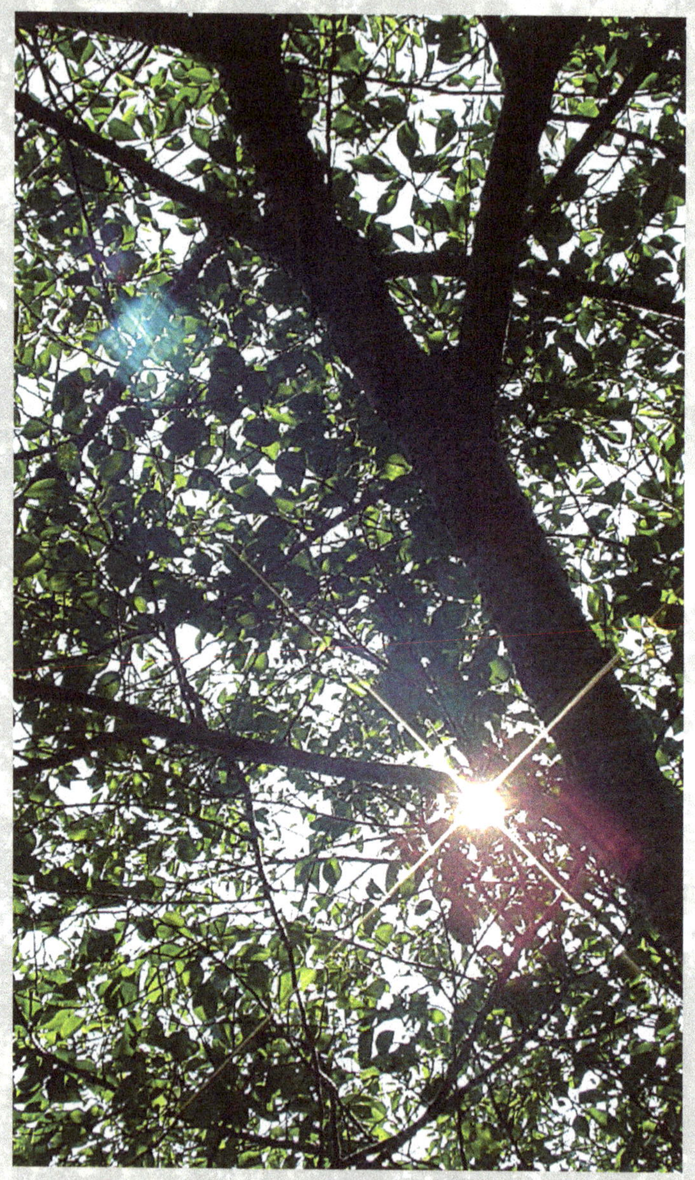

LOOK UP!
Musings on the Nature of Mindfulness

ESSAYS :: POEMS :: PHOTOGRAPHS
by Jennifer A. Payne

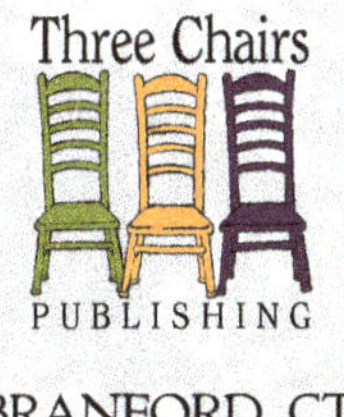

Three Chairs
PUBLISHING

BRANFORD, CT

©2014, 2024 by Jennifer A. Payne, text, photography, and artwork unless otherwise noted.

All rights reserved. No part of this book may be reproduced or translated in any form or by any means, digital, electronic, or mechanical, including photocopying, recording or by any information storage and retrieval system, without permission in writing from the publisher.

Book design by Jen Payne, Words by Jen. Body text is set in Chaparral Pro by Carol Twombly. Decorative font, Landsdowne, is by font designer Paul Lloyd. Cover font is True Golden by David Nalle (and William Morris).

ISBN: 978-0-9905651-0-9

THREE CHAIRS PUBLISHING
P.O. Box 453
Branford, CT 06405

www.threechairspublishing.com

Printed by IngramSpark in the U.S.A.

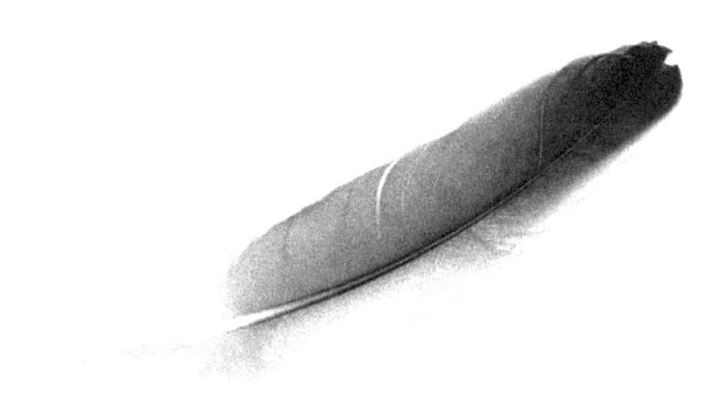

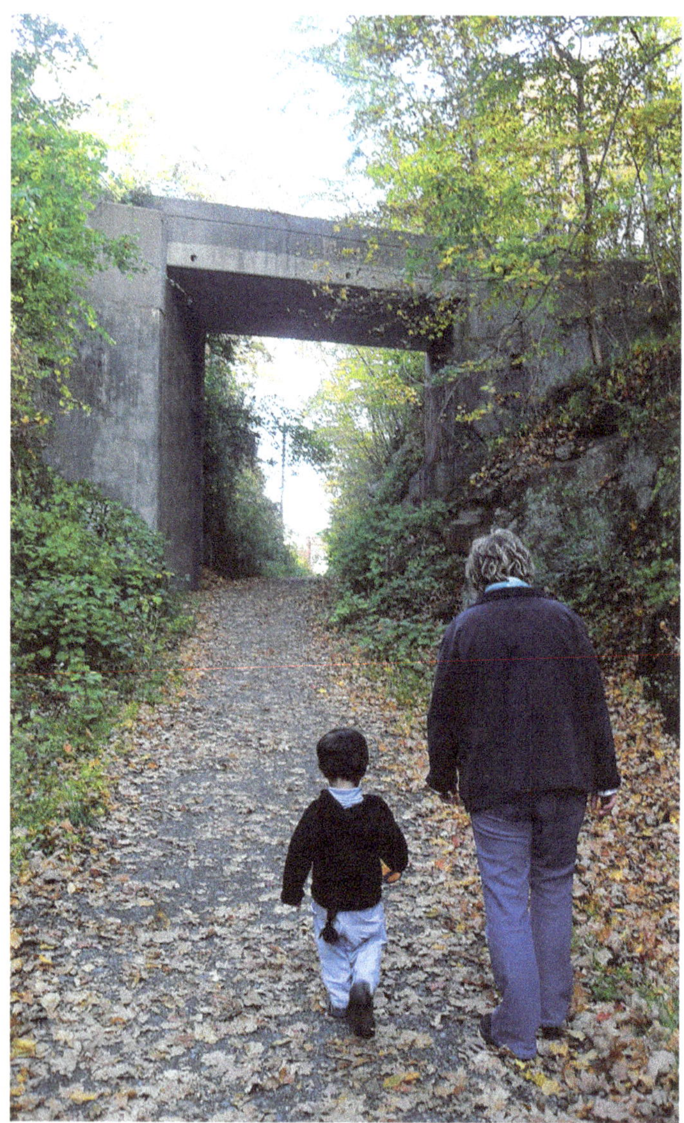

:: DEDICATION

For my Dad, who shows up in spirit as hawk.

For Rhonda, who sees and believes so effortlessly.

For Dale, who started this conversation before
I was ready—do you hear me talking with you?

And for Max—may you always remember to look up!

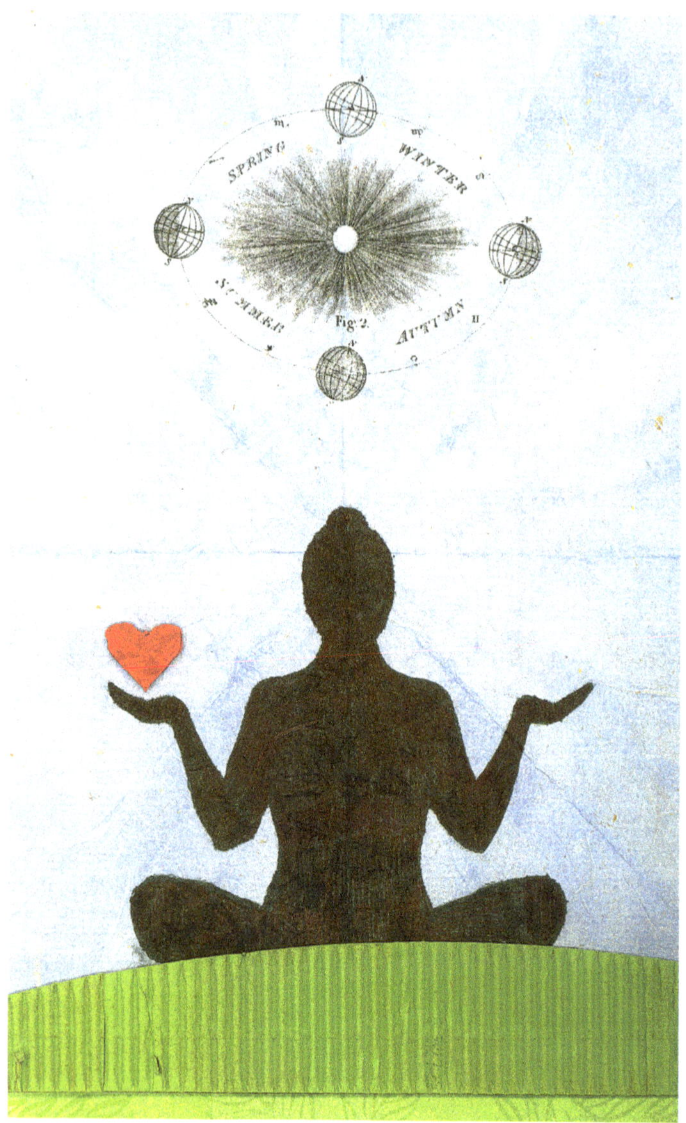
SPRING
WINTER
SUMMER
AUTUMN
Fig. 2.

:: WITH LOVE & THANKS

To Martha Link Walsh, my constant and confidant, who first introduced me to Ted Andrews' *Animal Speak* and opened a door to magic. It is a blessing to share this journey with you—daily.

To Mary O'Connor, fellow writer, poet, book author, Nature lover, and sounding board, for her ongoing counsel in all matters of the written word—including the first small seeds of this book.

To Peter Borgemeister, environmentalist and force of Nature, for the "windshield tour" that helped me see the world in a new way. I miss you, my friend.

To DeLinda Spain, my soul mate on the other end of this beautiful green ribbon; to Mary Anne Siok, my brazen, courageous sister who leads by example; to Melissa Cherry and the ever-present blessing of your spirit; and to Judith Bruder, for the gift of heartfelt conversations.

To Greg Sammons, my stalwart litmus test, photography wizard, and partner in the crime that is our daily effort of self-sustenance.

To my family—my Dad, my Mom, my Sister—who always allowed room for creativity, imagination and make-believe.

To Virginia Foster, friend and proofreader extraordinaire, for your fastidious review of my manuscript, your commitment to style, and the camaraderie of wordsmithing.

To Derek at Vashon Island Books (Vashon, Washington), who ended my two-month search for Hans Margolius and graciously sent photos as proof.

To Carrie Bergman for your enthusiastic contribution
of *The Tree of Contemplative Practices* from The Center
for Contemplative Mind in Society in Northampton,
Massachusetts.

To Jeff Cramer at the Thoreau Institute at Walden Woods
for your counsel on all things Thoreau.

To the folks at Hay House Publishing who gave me
permission to use their material with the following
blessing: "We are proud to extend our commitment
to individual and global enlightenment, and sincerely
thank you for contributing to our goals. Our audience is
concerned with our planet [and] the healing properties of
love...." *Amen.*

:: CONTENTS

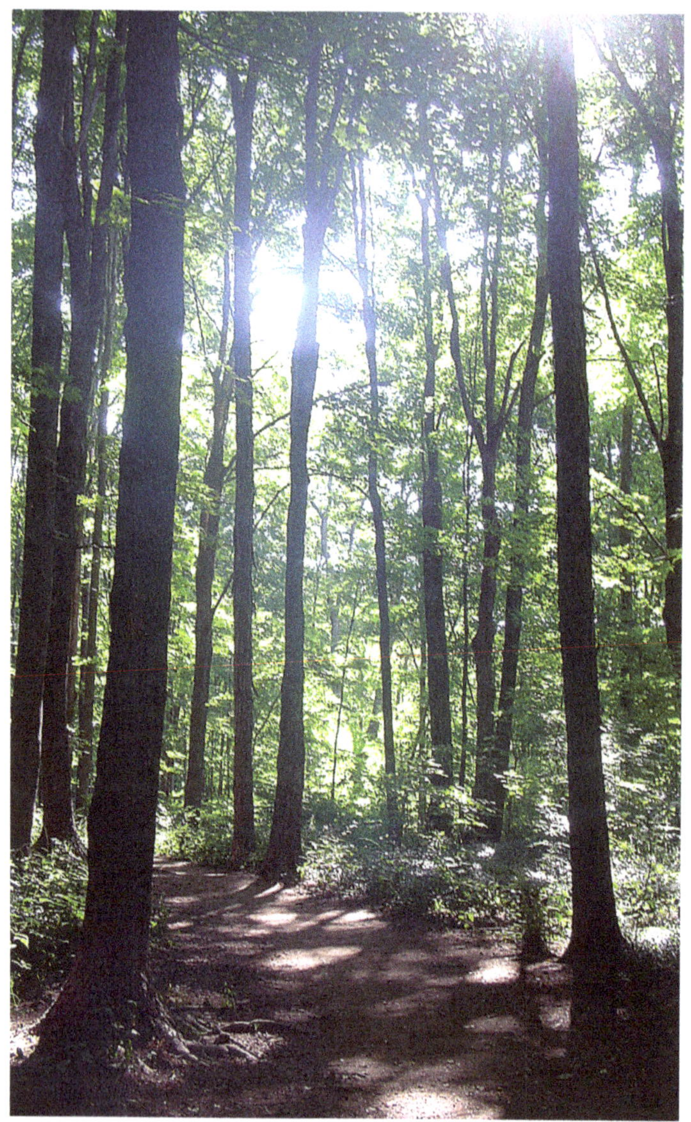

:: PREFACE

Random Acts of Writing and the
Happy Accident of Kindred Spirits

There are days in the woods when I walk for miles without seeing a soul—without the telltale approach of footsteps or the fleeting greetings as we pass. My discernible companions are only the birds overhead, the sound of my breath, and the shadows on the dappled trail.

And yet, I am never alone. There on the path in front of me walk kindred spirits—philosophers, poets, naturalists, writers. I am always surprised when they show themselves to me, when they call out and speak a language I have come to understand. No matter the distance, the differences, the dialect—in the woods, we all understand.

From the sacred texts of *The Dhammapada* and the poetry of Emily Dickinson, to the writings of Henry David Thoreau and the teachings of Jon-Kabat Zinn, there is a common thread that weaves together our encounters with Nature. The more I walk, the more I understand and desire to learn what each of them has to teach me.

In the beginning, I had no inclination to be a naturalist, nor was I on a spiritual journey—*a la sainte terre* as Albert Palmer writes in *The Mountain Trail and Its Message*[1]—but that is where I ended up. That is the consequence of opening our hearts to Nature, a deeper appreciation for the tangible and intangible elements of this place we call home.

My blog, *Random Acts of Writing*[2], from which this book was created, began as a way to share my creative writing efforts. Gradually, over time, its focus became more often about Nature and the walks I took in local parks and preserves. Those walks soon became my inspiration—for my writing, for my thoughts, for my quest to find more balance and peace in my life.

The encounters with the like-minded individuals mentioned above appeared as happy accidents—written treasures that communicated a moment better and more poetically than I could. That is, after all, why we quote famous people, is it not?

Woven, then, in between the essays and poems of *LOOK UP!*, you'll meet these kindred spirits; the ones you might expect, like naturalists Henry Beston, John Burroughs, Rachel Carson, John Muir, and Thoreau. But others you might not, like personal development teachers Dr. Wayne Dyer and Marianne Williamson. Included are beloved writers like Elizabeth Barrett Browning, Robert Frost, Rainer Maria

Rilke, and Walt Whitman—each one expressing his or her own thoughts on the confluence of Nature and something more magical.

From ancient texts like the Bible to contemporary spiritual teachers like Krishnamurti and the Dalai Lama, from the writings of Shakespeare to 20th- and 21st-century authors, naturalists, artists and bloggers—here on these pages you will come to understand the vast and wonderful lessons to be learned in the natural world.

There are, for sure, those tangible lessons about the Earth, its seasons and inhabitants: scientific ways of seeing, Latin names to research and remember, patterns and habits to study. But there are other lessons, too, about life, breath, mindfulness, balance, spirit. You can find them in books, most certainly, or sitting in yoga posture or prayer.

But you can also find them easily and spontaneously by taking a walk with Nature and the kindred spirits you meet along the way. The journey awaits you.

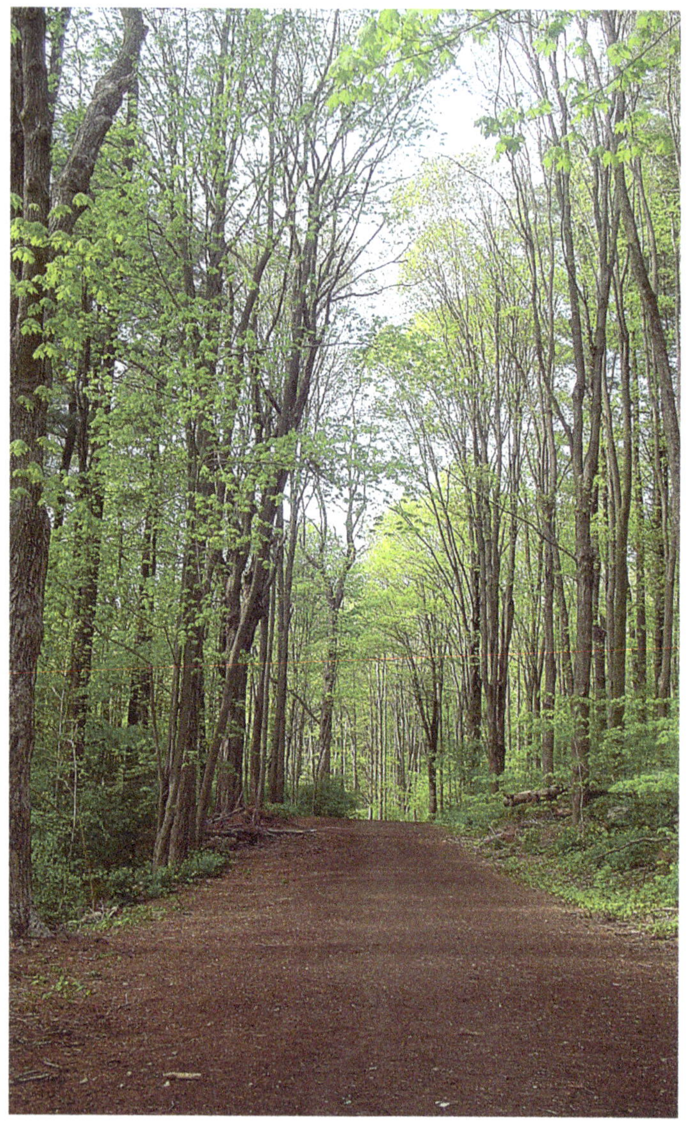

:: INTRODUCTION

The Journey

When I was nine years old, my little sister married Michael Greenberg in a beautiful meadow. She wore a string of plastic, emerald-colored beads and carried a seasonal bouquet of fleabane, Queen Anne's lace and goldenrod.

The meadow was a short walk away from the stone castle where I danced on moss carpet and ate raspberries picked from prickly branches. A visit to Pete's Pond revealed makeshift footbridges and a rope swing that reminded me of the fun house on the boardwalk in Wildwood, New Jersey. I liked to pretend that's where I was.

ONE OF MY FAVORITE SIGHTS, THE ENTRANCE TO THE WOODS. Look carefully and you'll see four versions in the book, one for each season, spring (seen here), summer (pg. 146), fall (pg. 46), and winter (pg. 114)

We lived, at the time, in a small apartment complex near a big city. The meadow—actually unmowed wildness beneath power lines—the castle, and Pete's Pond were in a small woodlot just a 10-minute walk from a giant strip mall that housed the A&P, a movie theater, and Toys"R"Us. But somehow, Nature found its way into my imagination...and into my heart.

When I was in fifth grade, we moved to a small shoreline town in Connecticut. One of my favorite books at the time was Gertrude Chandler Warner's *The Boxcar Children*. When I played in the woods behind our house, down the slope to the marsh, near the old well, I pretended I was like the Alden children—living in the woods, eating wild blueberries for supper, and making cool things from found objects.

Back then, there was always time to go play—in the backyard or behind the school where an endless maze of trails looped around a small pond. The town beach was a short bike ride away, and I spent time there, too—catching hermit crabs on the shore, collecting shells and sea glass, and bushwhacking through marsh grass.

But then things changed. A driver's license allowed access to something more efficient than a bike. Long walks to classes across campus replaced time to actually *play* outside. And life in the working world offered its own endless maze that didn't lead back to Nature for a very long time.

That's not to say Nature and I didn't keep in touch. I still enjoyed an occasional walk outside. Living in the shoreline town of Branford, Connecticut allowed for easy access to local beaches—if I were so inclined. Some of my favorite vacations were visits to the pristine White Mountains in New Hampshire. As a matter of fact, it was one such trip that inspired me to get involved with the local land trust.

I was introduced to the Branford Land Trust in 1994 by its then-president, Peter Borgemeister, a local environmentalist and force of Nature. Through Peter, I learned about Branford's wildlife, native and non-native species, and the importance of protecting open space—areas of land saved from development. I was thrilled to know that the Trust owned hundreds of acres of open space, and was actively involved in its maintenance and preservation. After one of Peter's famous "windshield tours" of town, I became a volunteer. I wrote press releases for Land Trust fundraisers, designed their newsletter and website, and spent more than 10 years promoting their preservation efforts. All while never setting foot on one trail or property.

At the time, I was busy establishing my own business. I worked 10- and 12-hour days, six or seven days a week. I rarely took days off, and what free time I did have I spent volunteering and attending committee meetings.

And then things changed. Again.

I often refer to the time around my 40th birthday as the "Year of Great Transition." A failed romance and a health crisis shifted a fault line, sending tremors in every facet of my life—my work, my dreams, my relationships. Everything felt suddenly out of balance. But the truth of the matter was, everything had been out of balance for a long time, and it took a little earth shaking for me to realize I needed to make some changes.

It was about that time that my dear and oldest friend Rhonda and I went for a walk along the Trolley Trail. It's a beautiful path that winds its way through a lush salt marsh, across a boardwalk, past giant granite outcrops, to an old trolley bridge that overlooks one of Connecticut's most scenic harbors.

As we walked, it was hard to miss her fascination with everything around us. An artist and long-time naturalist, she seemed so inspired and awestruck. She knew the names of the shorebirds that glided above us and recognized the call of the osprey from its nest. She knew the flow of the tide from the smell of the air. She noticed the details, like the multitude of colors reflecting in the water.

And suddenly I realized—so did I! I knew Egret and Heron! I recognized Honeysuckle and Black-Eyed Susan! I knew the smell of a birch branch when snapped in half and the feel of the cool moss hiding in cracks along the granite!

It was like walking into a room full of faces and suddenly realizing you know everyone. There were old friends from summer camp and Girl Scouts. There were ones I met along the Delaware River at my grandfather's fishing cabin and at the campground my family stayed at in Maine. There were friends I knew from the town beach and friends from that magical forest I played in when I was nine.

It was a clarion call to look up, to get up, to get out. After that day with Rhonda, I started to walk more—at the Trolley Trail, in the parcel of open space across from my house, around the pond at the nature preserve on the other side of town. Whenever a break in my routine presented itself, I went walking…until walking became part of the routine.

Gradually, over the weeks and months, a new awareness unfolded for me that was foreign but familiar, quiet but life-changing.

What follows is a journal of that unfolding—told through my own essays, poems, and photographs, as well as quotations and writing from kindred spirits such as Henry David Thoreau, Emily Dickinson, John Muir, and Walt Whitman. I use the word *journal* because what follows was originally published on my personal blog, *Random Acts of Writing*, over the course of several years. The entries were selected to be part of *LOOK UP!* because of the collective story they tell.

The word *journal* also seems appropriate because it shares its roots with the word *journey*, and, as you will see, this has indeed been a journey. When I finally learned to look up— from the work, the distractions, the routines—I found my way back to that spirit who loved to play outside, who was curious about her surroundings, whose imagination knew no boundaries.

When I finally learned to look up, I found much more— peace, solace, joy, *connection*.

I hope you find the same within these pages, and in your own corner of this magical world in which we are blessed to live.

With Love, Jen

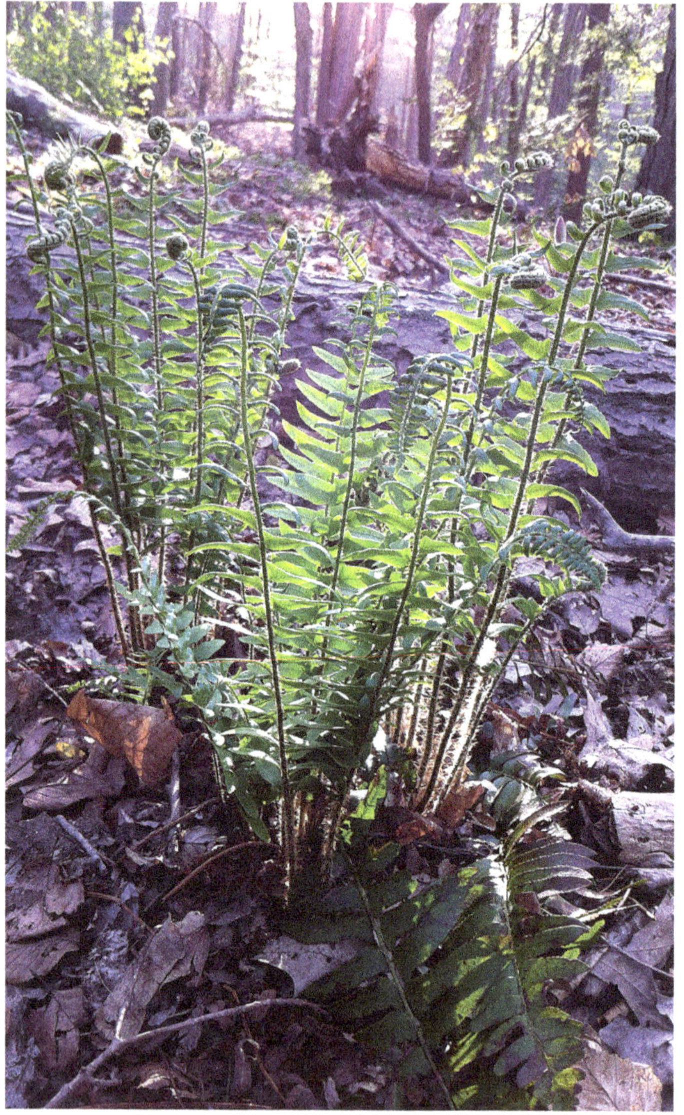

Getting Out

"What is this?" I asked the guide who led the

   early spring hike.

"And this?"

"Is that a heron?" I pointed up to the sky.

My curiosity was brimming.

"What is this?" my bare arms asked the warmth of the sun.

"And that?" my hair wondered at the breeze.

We wondered all spring.

"Can this be true?" my nose questioned the flowers.

"How does this feel?" sought my toes in the ocean.

"Where does that go?" asked my eyes to the trail up ahead.

"And how have I missed this before?"

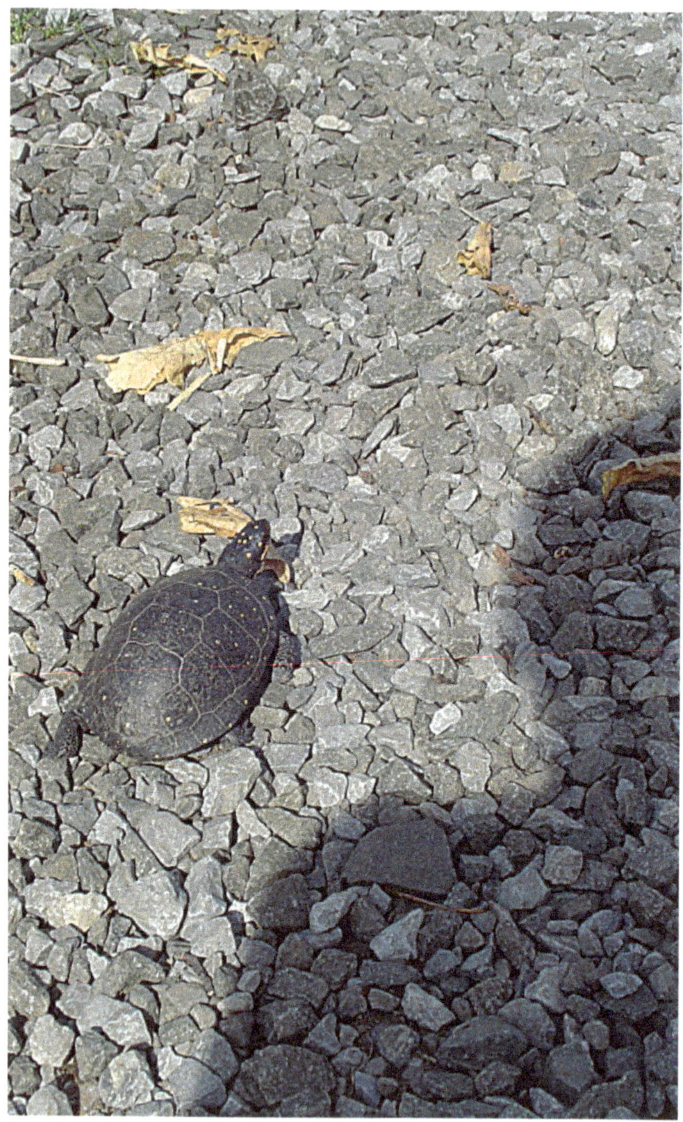

Close Encounter

"Rise up, my love, my fair one, and come away.

For, lo, the winter is past, the rain is over and gone.

The flowers appear on the earth; the time of the

singing of birds is come, and the voice of the turtle

is heard in our land."

— Song of Solomon 2:10-12 (KJV)[3]

SPOTTED TURTLE

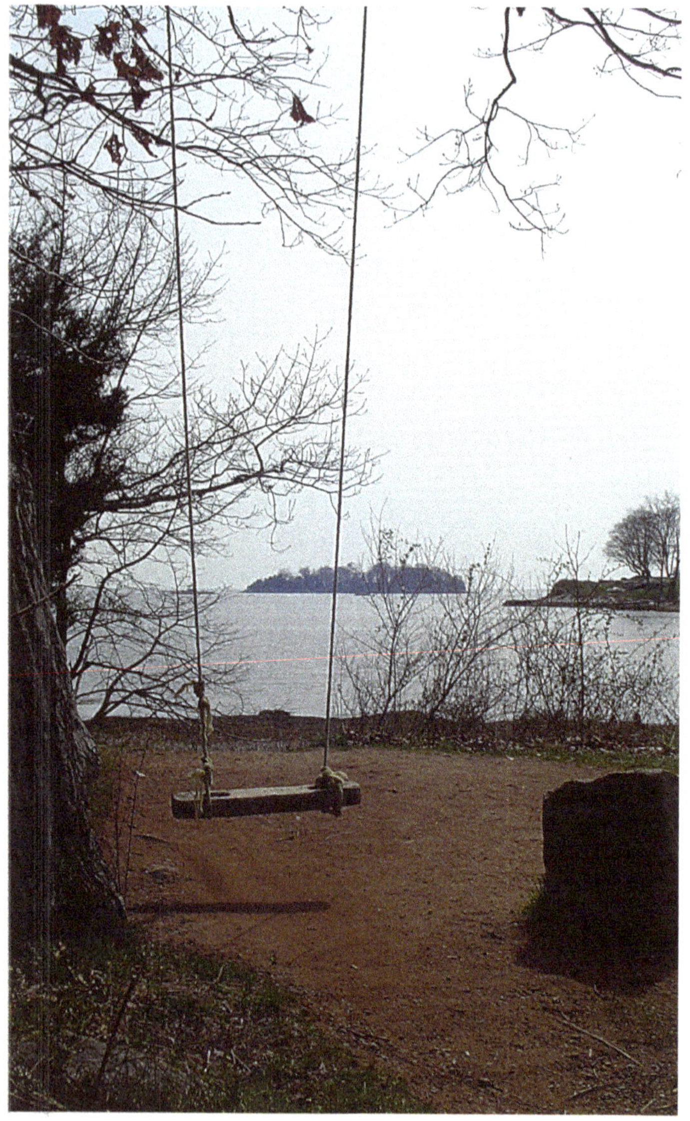

Thank You, Attilio Banca

I am blessed. That was the conclusion I came to at the end of a day that started at 5:00 a.m. with no cream for my coffee, followed by back-to-back appointments with anxious clients, an infinite To Do list, and a jumble of phone calls and emails.

But there I was, ten hours later, walking. Walking in short sleeves, mind you, on the most glorious summer day to ever eavesdrop into April!

The sky was blue, the birds were in symphony, and an osprey couple surveyed their new nest. A breeze blew in from the south, shepherding smells of the sea and the calls of gulls. Four teenage boys were diving off a bridge into high-tide water in a surreal sort of Huck-Finnian moment.

There was all of that and me, swinging back and forth on a makeshift swing hanging from winter-bare branches in a clearing overlooking a tidal marsh and Long Island Sound.

A plaque nearby noted that the marsh was donated in memory of Attilio J. Banca.

According to a *Hartford Courant* article[4], more than 90 years ago, young Attilio met a World War I veteran who was convalescing at a home in Stony Creek, Connecticut. Attilio and Jules Andre Smith, an artist, author, and architect, became fast friends. Near the marsh, they built an art studio and gallery, which Attilio ran for many years.

I have no doubt that Attilio witnessed similar days as this. Perhaps even he leisurely swung on a swing in a clearing overlooking this same marsh—letting his worries be carried north with the wind.

I have no doubt he, like I, could make his way home then, knowing "I am blessed."

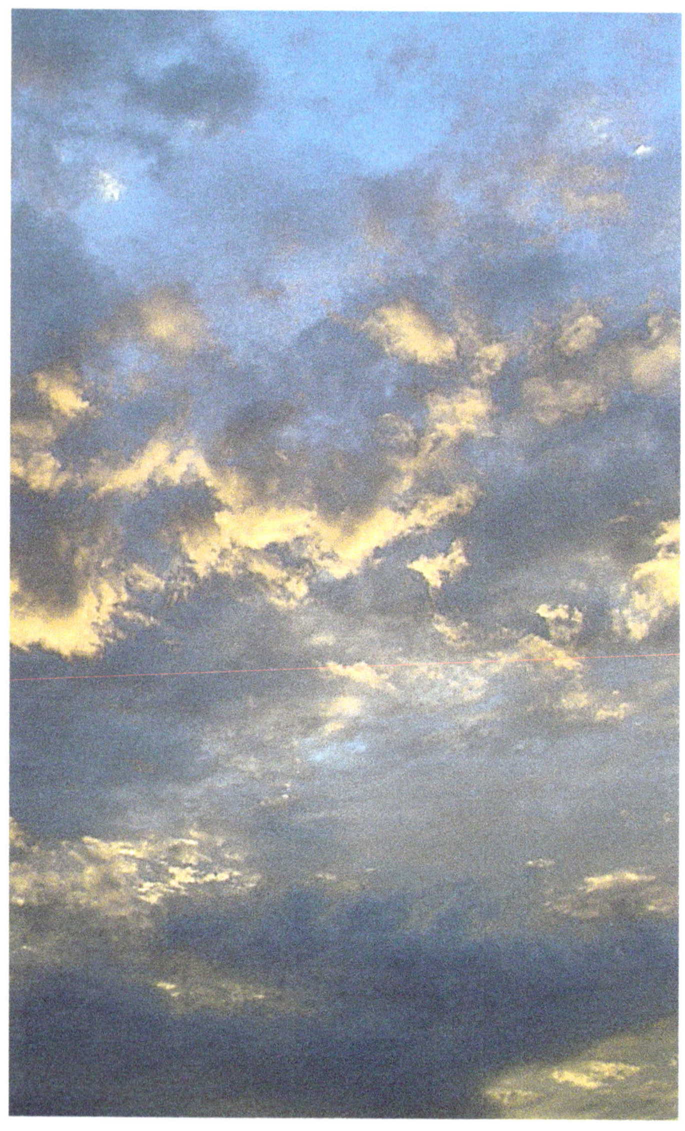

Change of Heart

"When I heard the learn'd astronomer,

When the proofs, the figures, were ranged in columns
before me,

When I was shown the charts and diagrams, to add,
divide, and measure them,

When I sitting heard the astronomer where he lectured
with much applause in the lecture-room,

How soon unaccountable I became tired and sick,

Till rising and gliding out I wander'd off by myself,

In the mystical moist night-air, and from time to time,

Look'd up in perfect silence at the stars."

— Walt Whitman, "When I Heard the Learn'd Astronomer"[5]

More than 100 years after Whitman, Rachel Carson wrote *The Sense of Wonder*, encouraging parents to take their children outside, to see for themselves the abundance of Nature, to experience the power of discovery, to stare—as Whitman notes—"in perfect silence at the stars."

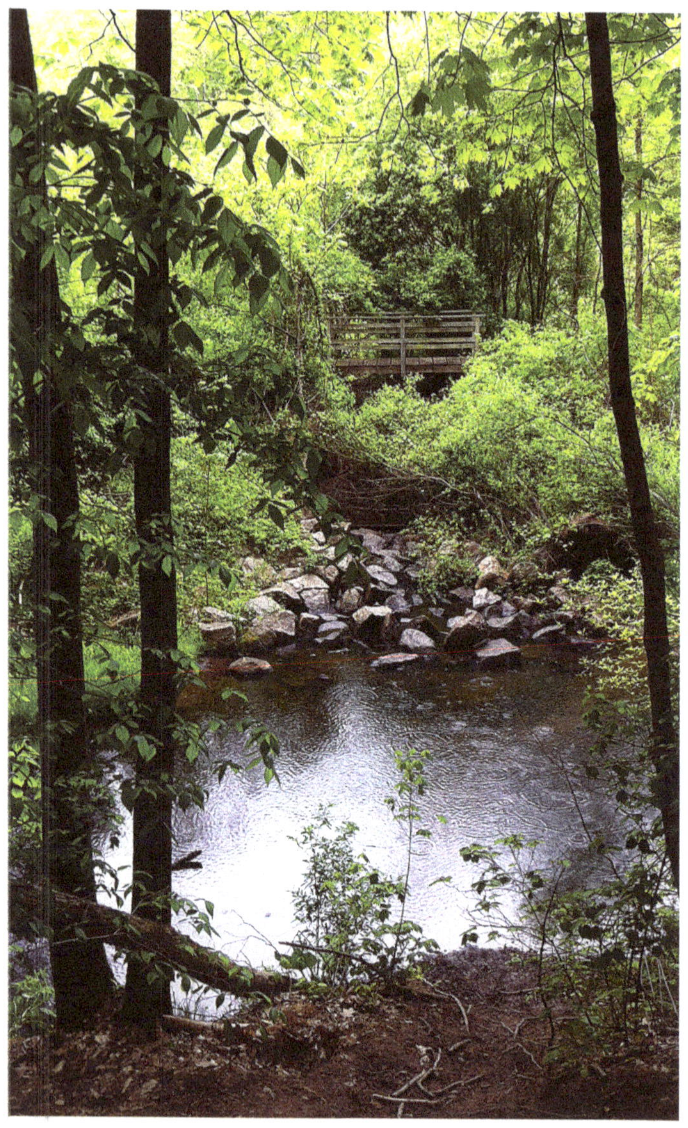

:: JUNE

Gone Walking

"Now shall I walk

or shall I ride?

'Ride,' Pleasure said.

'Walk,' Joy replied."

— William H. Davies[6]

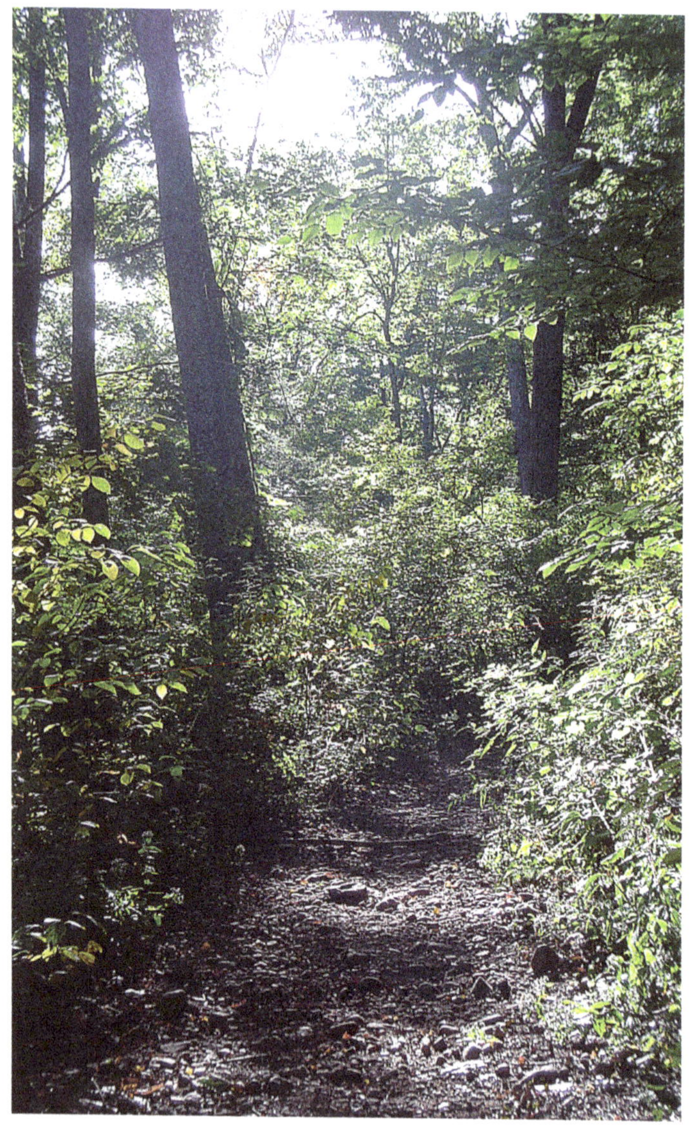

A Meditation on Bugs

A wicked storm blew through Connecticut today. While there was tornado-like damage to the west, we survived with a brief but torrential downpour and some hardy wind gusts. As it passed, the August-like heat of the day subsided just enough that it seemed like a good time for a walk.

But I forgot about the bugs.

I hadn't walked five minutes up the trail before they ambushed me. A swarm of gnats dropped down in front of my face like a thin, black veil. Two flies laid claim to my ears—bzzzzzzzzzzzzing in stereo. Their siege left me breathless—afraid to inhale the little creatures.

My swatting—*swat, buzz, swat, buzz, swat, buzz, buzz!*—was moot.

By coincidence, I had recently watched a scene from the movie *Eat Pray Love*[7] in which the Julie Roberts character successfully sits in meditation for a full hour despite an enthusiastic swarm of bugs and thoughts. She lets the small annoyances pass and finds her way to stillness.

That's not me.

I'm still dancing with meditation, and it's no waltz. More like the fifties' stroll, with me lined up on this side and meditation way over there on that side.

Last winter, I went to a guided group meditation. A kind and creative soul gently guided us for an hour. We floated through the sky, over the ocean, into the stars—okay, THEY floated. I spent the entire hour imagining myself running after them, trying to catch up!

The truth is, I don't sit still. I don't, and my mind doesn't either. We're always running after something—the next project, the next errand, the next idea. Lots and lots of thoughts...like the lots and lots of bugs around my head!

This similarity did not escape me.

In her book *Stop the Pain: Adult Meditations*, my dear friend Dale Carlson explains that there are many ways to meditate: "If your nervous system is the result of an active gene pool or you are personally too frayed to sit down right off, begin with a walk."[8]

My walks have become my meditation, so today was particularly challenging. I wanted to find my way to quiet. I tried to just be with the bugs. I walked (swat), I listened to the birds (buzz), I looked up at the trees (swat), I heard the leaves rustle (buzz).

Over and over again, I tried to bring my mind back to the present—to "pay attention" as Dale often reminds me—walking on a trail, drops of rain on my head, the smell of damp earth. And over and over again, my mind would run after the bugs.

But I am learning to let these annoyances pass over me. There are days, like today, when the bugs stay with me, buzzing their demands and nipping at my spirit for the entire walk.

And then there are days I walk with great ease—my breath is free, my mind is clear, and everything around me glows.

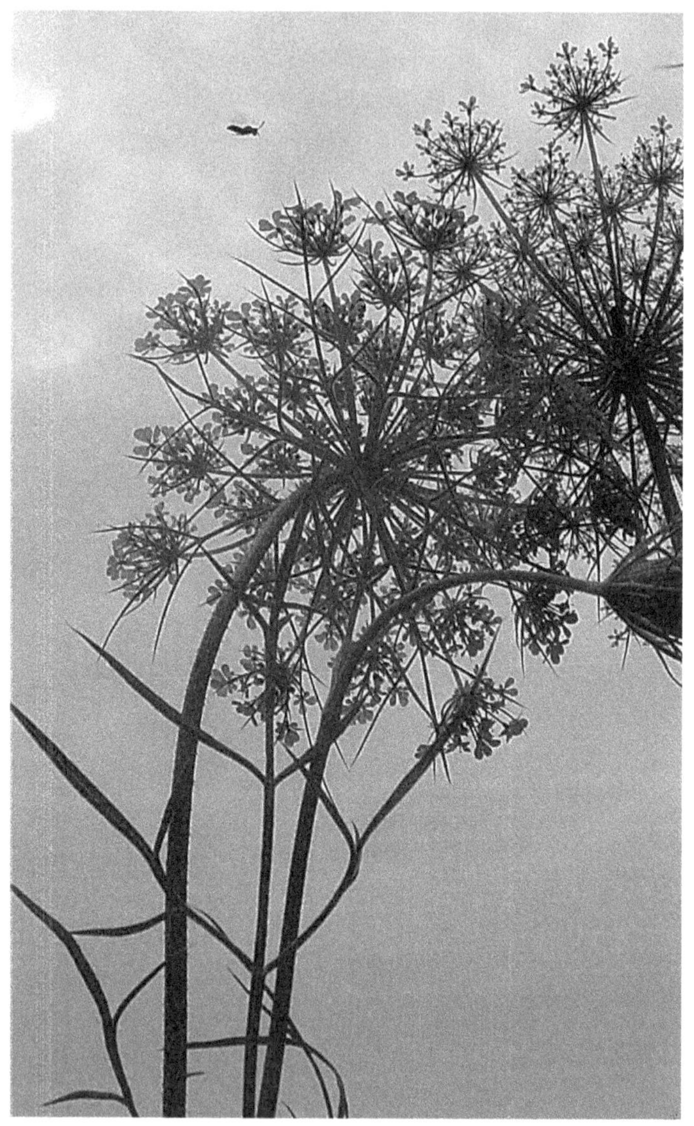

A Great Opportunity

"It takes a long time for the Puritan work ethic mind to discover that one is the most productive when the mind and the shoulders are at ease, that focusing outward in disciplined observation allows the mind the greatest inner opportunity to create and to play."

— Ann Zwinger, *The Naturalist's Path*[9]

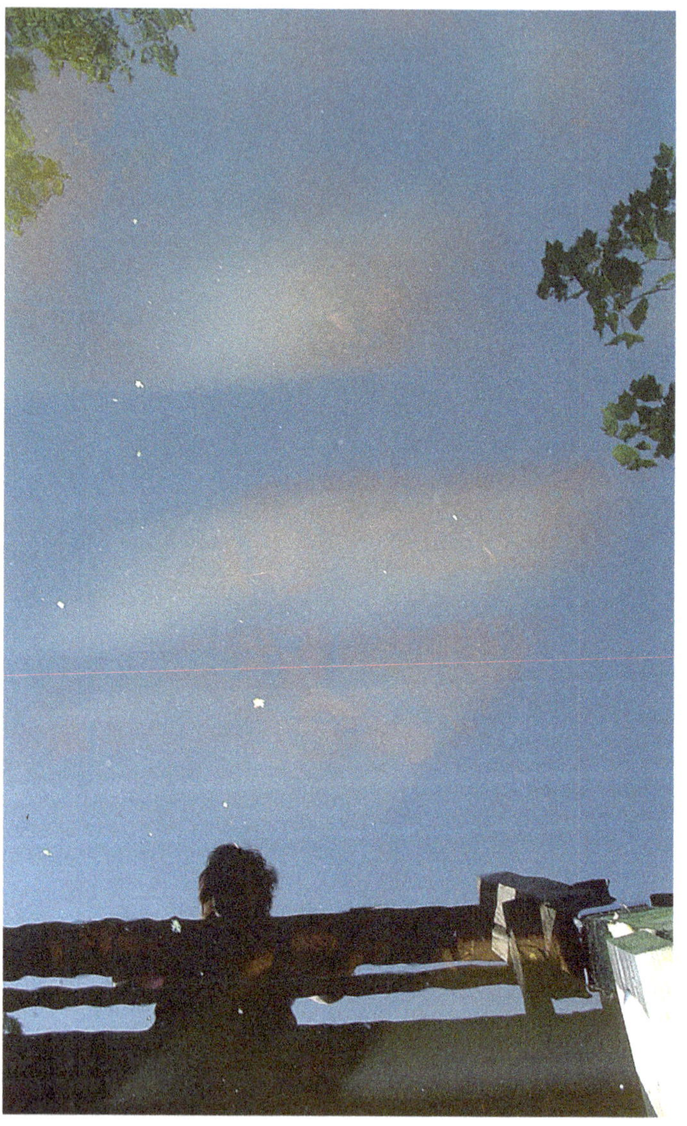

What Business Have I Here if I Am Elsewhere?

"I am alarmed when it happens that I have walked a mile into the woods bodily, without getting there in spirit. In my afternoon walk I would fain forget all my morning occupations and my obligations to society. But it sometimes happens that I cannot easily shake off the village. The thought of some work will run in my head and I am not where my body is,—I am out of my senses. In my walks I would fain return to my senses. What business have I in the woods, if I am thinking of something out of the woods?"

— Henry David Thoreau, "Walking"[10]

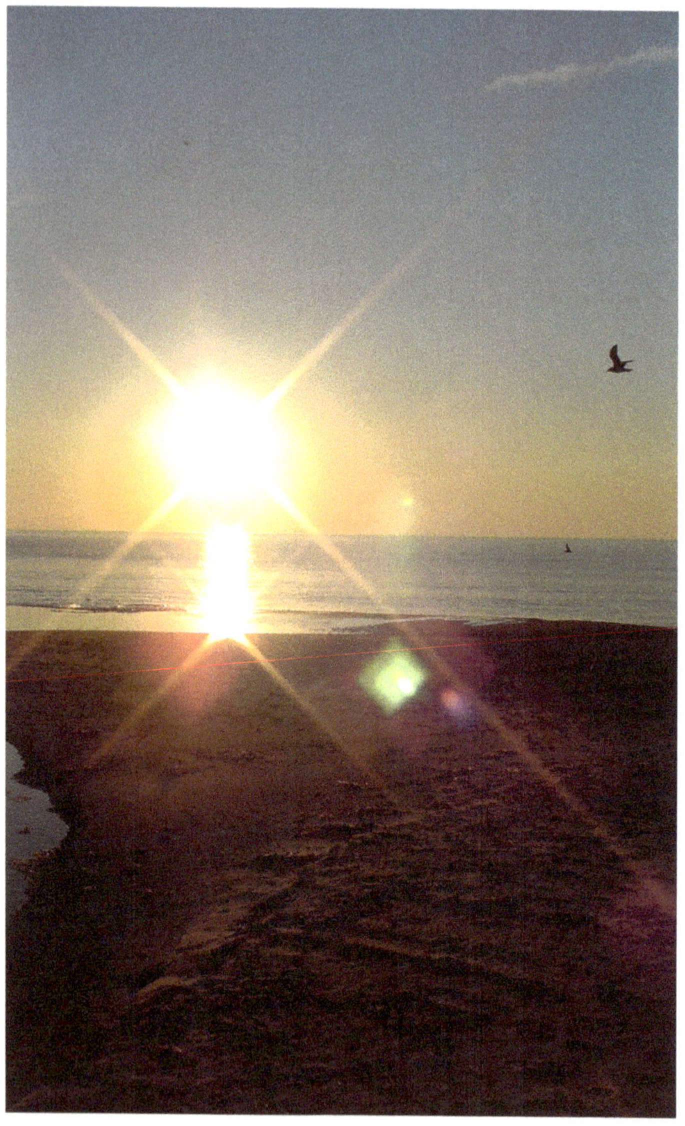

:: JULY

Losing My Religion

"Dad's not there," my sister responded adamantly, when I suggested we go back to the cemetery the night of his funeral.

I don't know how, or if, she'd found such clarity about it. I was four years older with five years of therapy under my belt, and I couldn't say much of anything with clarity. Except that my father was dead.

So, *where* was he?

Physically, I knew he was in the casket. Spiritually was a whole other matter. *Where was he?*

At the time of his death, I still referred to myself as "Catholic." Loosely. The answer to "where?" was just as loose—heaven? cosmic dust? ghost?

During his eulogy, I read the famous quote: "What lies behind us and what lies before us are but tiny matters compared to what lies within us."[11] I knew my Dad was *in* me, a part of me, as sure as I knew he was in the casket. I was his daughter, had his sense of humor, his work ethic.

That night, at the cemetery, I sat alone at the gravesite. The heavenly scent of funeral flowers hung in the air, and a glorious sunset cast wide rays of golden light across the sky. At that moment, Dad was there. With me. Saying goodbye.

Whether by myself in attempted prayer or with others in rote memorial, my subsequent visits to his gravesite left me feeling detached and empty. *Where was he?*

It would be 15 years before I again found that connection with my father.

As I stood there a few weeks ago, it occurred to me that much had changed. The learned exercise of genuflection and prayer seemed foreign, associated with religious designations I'd let go of long ago. My heart—my spirit— was looser now, and with that freedom came connection.

Instead of offering up some peripheral prayer or filling the void with rambling, I looked for the quiet. I sat at his grave, put both palms flat out on the grass, and closed my eyes. I felt the breeze blow through my hair. I smelled the Pennsylvania dirt, rich with minerals. I sensed the dampness of the ground beneath me.

Then, in the distance, a raven called out from a nearby tree, penetrating the thin veil of silence.

As is my effort of late, I brought my attention back—to the breeze, the dirt, the dampness. But with each attempt, there was the raven and his ever-present calling.

When I finally stood up, I realized the raven had quieted as soon as my eyes opened, and I knew this was no coincidence.

It was not the first time my father has appeared in this form for me. He has done so many times. An eagle, soaring overhead. A hawk, silently watching from its branch.

"I sense your father," an intuitive told me recently. "He's off in the distance a bit, but he wants you to know he's here for you."

"He says he loves you. He's proud of you," she said, pausing perplexed.

"But you knew that? Maybe that's why he's just sort of hovering. He knows you know that."

And I do. Every day.

When I think back to the day of my Dad's funeral, I often refer to it as both the worst day and the best day of my life. It was the worst, for obvious reasons. It was the best because it was the first day I ever felt connected to something greater and more wonderful.

I have ever since, I think. But I'm just now learning how to fly with it.

As a matter of fact, as I walked in the woods yesterday and wrote these words in my head, my Dad was with me. I heard his voice as clear as day and saw a magnificent hawk soaring above me, dancing along the treetops.

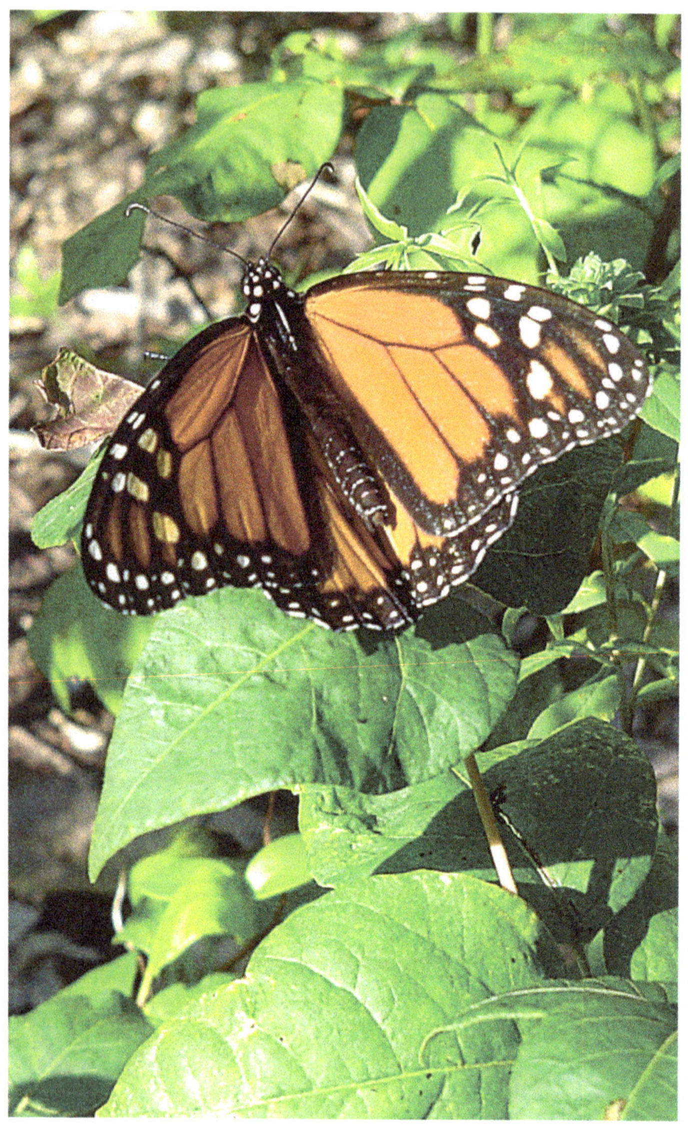

Pieces of Thought

"F"or every action there is an equal and opposite reaction,"[12] Isaac Newton said.

"You overcome old habits by leaving them behind,"[13] author Wayne Dyer said, some 300 years later.

I don't think either of them was talking about keys...but I am.

I was walking through the woods the other day, thinking about the things we carry with us. The physical things—like keys—and the less tangible, like memories. The things we carry with us can be heavy—grudges or a responsibility. Or they can be light—kind words or pieces of a poem.

The bee is not afraid of me,
I know the butterfly;
The pretty people in the woods
Receive me cordially.

— Emily Dickinson[14]

MONARCH

Often, the things we carry with us are no longer necessary.

For example, the key chain I carry holds 11 keys, three key fobs, and bar-coded tags for access to my library, AAA, and mile-long receipts from CVS.

Of those keys, I use three: house, car, post office box. One opens the door to a friend's house, but I can't remember the last time I used any of the other ones. That's seven keys—or about four ounces—I carry around with no purpose.

Imagine if the nontangible things carried weight as well? An ounce for that grudge, another for that resentment. Two ounces for that grief and two more for that heartache. Perhaps they do.

But can I leave them behind? I wonder as I walk. Can I let go of those old things that no longer serve a purpose? Can I overcome stale habits and welcome bright new ones?

If I want to change things, according to Newton, I must do something: every object tends to remain in its state of motion unless an external force is applied to it.

If I leave them behind, and there is an equal and opposite reaction, will I manifest positive change? What new doors will open? And won't I need a new key?

Some of my favorite things to carry with me are the beautiful words and melodies of John Denver—reminders of the days when I played with Nature as a child. When I am there, his songs are captions for what I see around me. When I am elsewhere, they call me back. Listen to the songs "Windsong" and "Spirit" and you might find a keepsake or two yourself.

Now Playing
For Mary

All the world's a stage," Shakespeare wrote in *As You Like It*. As I like it is a day like this...

Setting: a summer-green dais with sky-blue backdrop, framed by trees that sway with the warm summer breeze.

In the wings, a flurry of beachgoers and bullfrogs, herons and hummingbirds.

My friend Mary and I sitting center stage, meandering through creative conversations, as clouds and boats and birds enter and exit without cue.

...this our life exempt from public haunt,
Finds tongues in trees, books in the running brooks,
Sermons in stones, and good in every thing.[15]

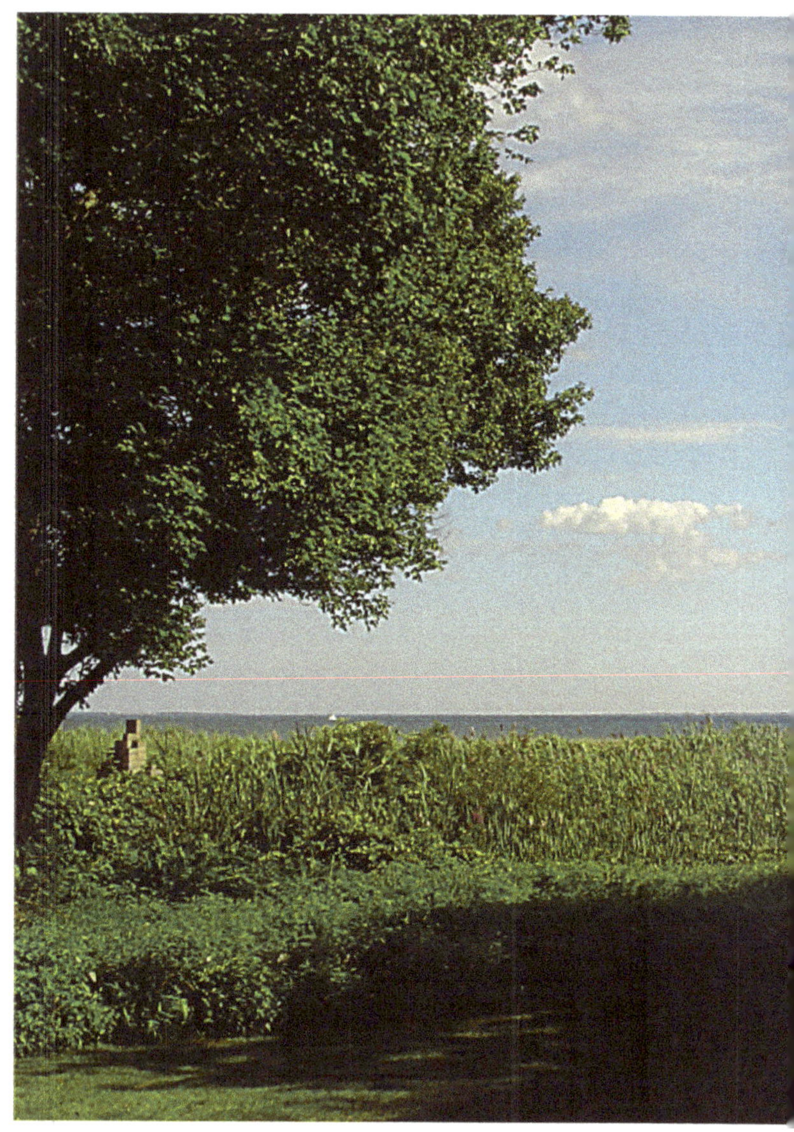

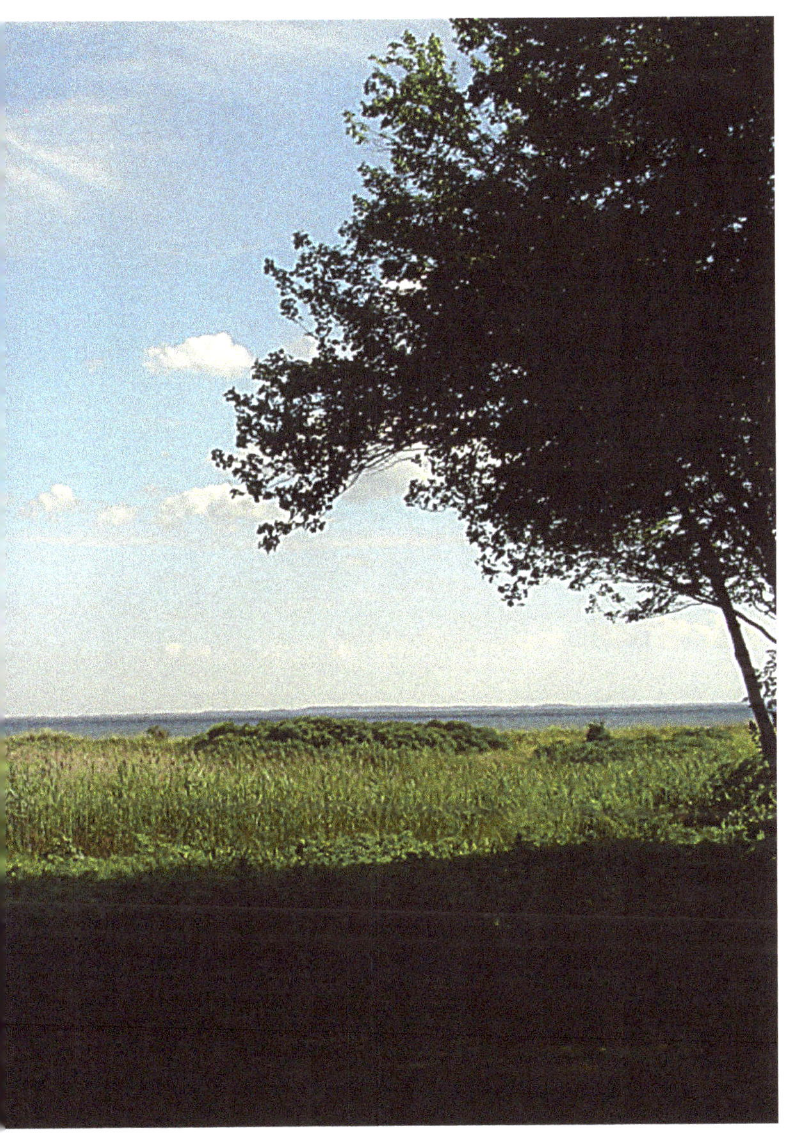

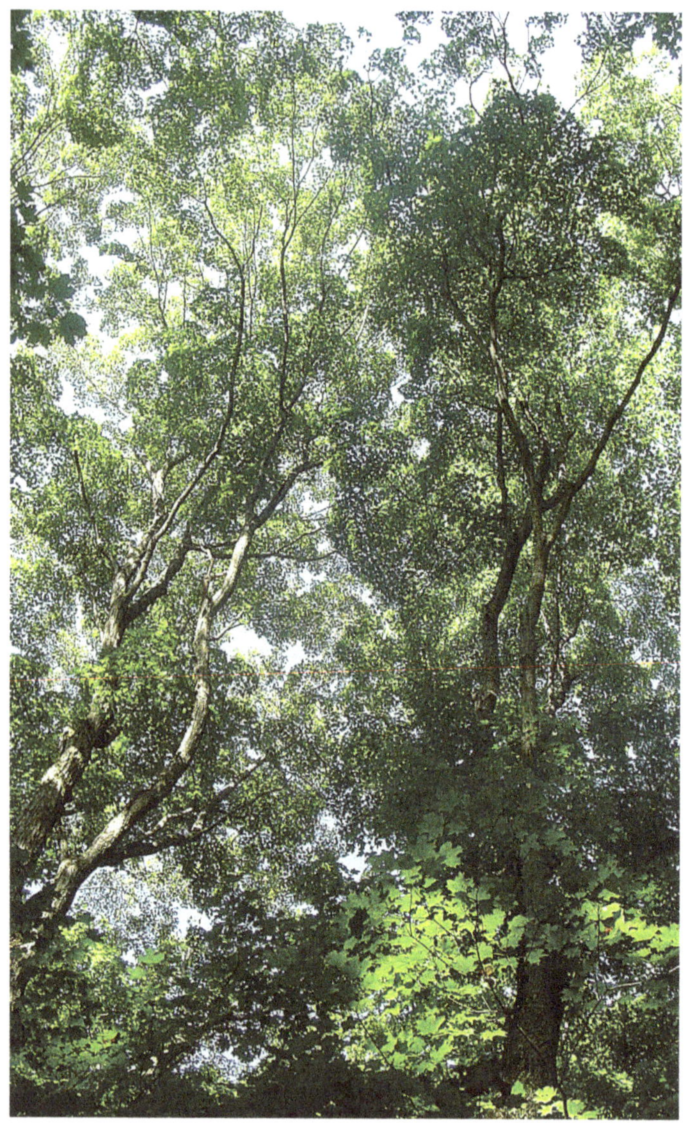

:: AUGUST

Sunday at the Park

You want me to what?

Lie here?

That's all?

No phone calls or emails?

No errands or chores?

No work or list of things to do?

Are you sure?

You just want me to

lie here on this blanket?

With that gift of a cool breeze

blowing in from the ocean?

And the sun sneaking through the branches

to dance across my skin?

You just want me to lie here?

And not do anything?

Seriously?

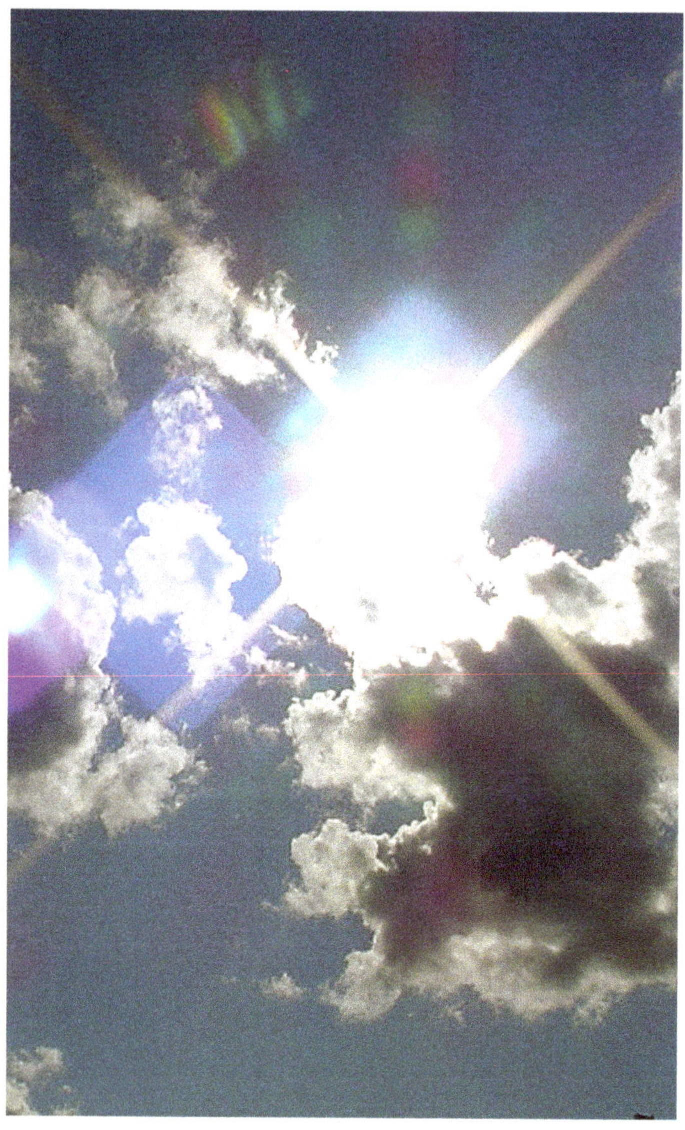

Left to Our Own Devices

"What are you doing?

I'm using my device.

What is your device?

My device is the sky.

Does your device have many applications?

Yes. It has the sun, moon, clouds and birds.

And do you have to recharge your device very often?

I don't ever have to recharge my device. It recharges me."

— Michael Leunig[16]

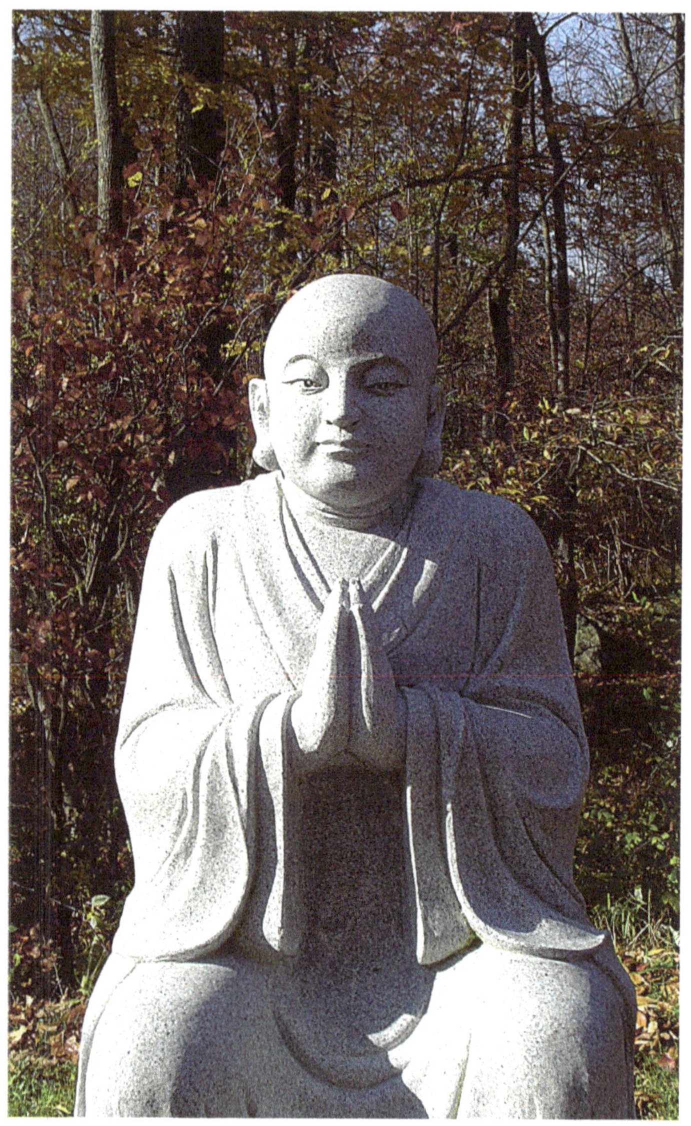

:: SEPTEMBER

Asking for Directions, Part I

When I was young I would pray for silly things: that I could stay up late to watch TV, that we would have pancakes for breakfast.

I also prayed a lot for boys—make him love me, make him not leave.

I prayed for world peace, because that's what you did. And I prayed for my grandmother—she needed someone on her side.

I remember the last time I prayed. Closing my eyes and repeating the words over and over—*please let him live, please let him live.*

He did not. And I stopped.

Praying, that is. I stopped praying. I assumed I wasn't doing it right. Or no one was listening.

For a long time after my Dad's death, the idea that "life is random" suited me just fine—no requests needed. And while I would "keep you in my thoughts," or "send you positive energy," I got out of the habit of praying. It—along with forgiveness, contrition, gratitude—got tossed into the pile of "raised Catholic" and forgotten.

PRAY 1. to make earnest petition to. 2. to offer devout petition, praise, thanks, etc., to (God or an object of worship). 3. to make petition or entreaty for; crave. 4. to offer (a prayer). 5. to ask, make request of.

In April, a psychic noted, "You have not reached out for spiritual support."

In June, a woman in my Sharing Circle echoed, "Just ask for guidance, it will come."

"Ask how?" I wanted to know. Surely not in the Please-God-Give-Me-Amen way I knew as a girl.

And ask what? If I don't know what I want, how can I ask for it?

But I've been practicing asking—albeit in a fairly noncommittal way. Picture Natalie Wood's half-hearted "I do believe. I do believe." in *Miracle on 34th Street*.

"Where do you want me to go?
What do you want me to do next?"

On a walk last week, I asked for guidance and got "let go of the fear."

In a dream, I was shown a silent Buddhist temple shrouded in incense.

"What is holding you back? What are you afraid of?" a friend asked last week.

"Sit in silence," something keeps nagging me, dropping words along my path: ritual, meditate, mindfulness.

Where do you want me to go? What do you want me to do next?

Stop being afraid and shut up.

This is my response.

Stop being afraid and shut up.

The Tree of
Contemplative Practices

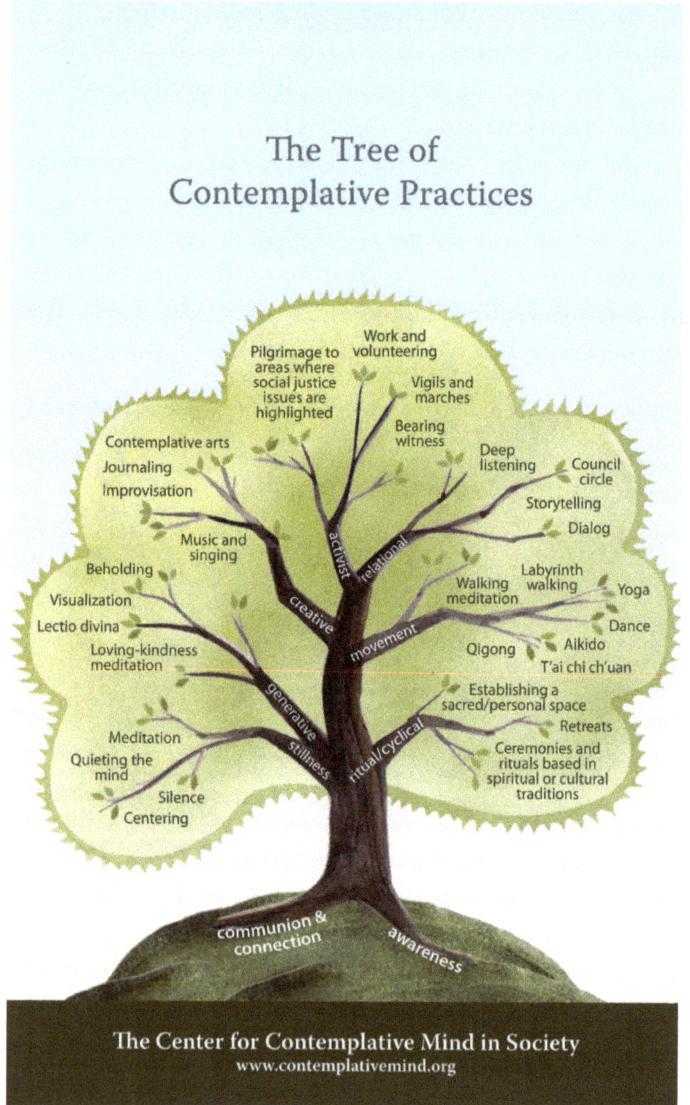

The Center for Contemplative Mind in Society
www.contemplativemind.org

Asking for Directions, Part II

Where do you want me to go? What do you want me to do next?" I ask the Universe.

"Stop being afraid and shut up," She tells me.

It's "shut up" in a kind way, don't get me wrong. (She sounds as if She's speaking Yiddish, actually.) And I know what She means. Even I get tired of the busy chatter that goes on in my head sometimes.

Yesterday, I was walking in the woods. It was a gorgeous, early fall day. The sun was warm, the breeze was cool, and my mind was chattering away—blah, blah, blah, blahblahblahblah. It was as spastic as the chipmunks giggling in the leaves along the trail. When I finally realized I'd spent most of the walk in busy-brain mode, I stopped. Closed my eyes and tried to quiet the prattle.

Breathe.

One. Two. Three. Blah. Four. Blah. Five. Blah. Blah. Blah.

Ahem.

One. Two. Blah. Three. Blah. Four. Blah.

Argh!

"Sha! Shtil! Shhh," She says. "Quiet!"

"Where do you want me to go? What do you want me to do next?" I ask.

"Shut up," She repeats, kindly.

She knows I have trouble with this.

Which is why, perhaps, the sheet of paper at my client's office last week was oddly askew in its rack.

Which is why, perhaps, the colorful illustration caught my eye.

Which is why, perhaps, I picked it up and read *The Tree of Contemplative Practices*.[17]

"Shut up," She repeats, smiling.

The Tree of Contemplative Practices was created by Maia Duerr for The Center for Contemplative Mind in Society in Northampton, Massachusetts.

The illustration, by Carrie Bergman, shows a simple tree with roots firm in the earth and branches reaching up to the sky. The roots of the tree symbolize the intentions of contemplative practices: cultivating awareness and developing a stronger connection to the divine, or inner wisdom. The branches represent and illustrate different types of practices, including stillness, movement, creative, and generative. On the stillness branch, for example, the illustration presents silence, centering, meditation, quieting the mind.

"Shut up," She motions her head to the piece of paper askew, to the colorful illustration, to the words and soft guidance.

"Where do you want me to go? What do you want me to do next?" I ask the Universe.

And She responds.

If you visit the Center for Contemplative Mind in Society's website, www.contemplativemind.org, you'll find an entire section devoted to the concept of contemplative practices. In addition to broad descriptions of the concept, the site also includes information about many of the individual practices— articles, definitions, how-to instructions—as well as ways to begin a contemplative practice, how to find retreats, and recommended reading.

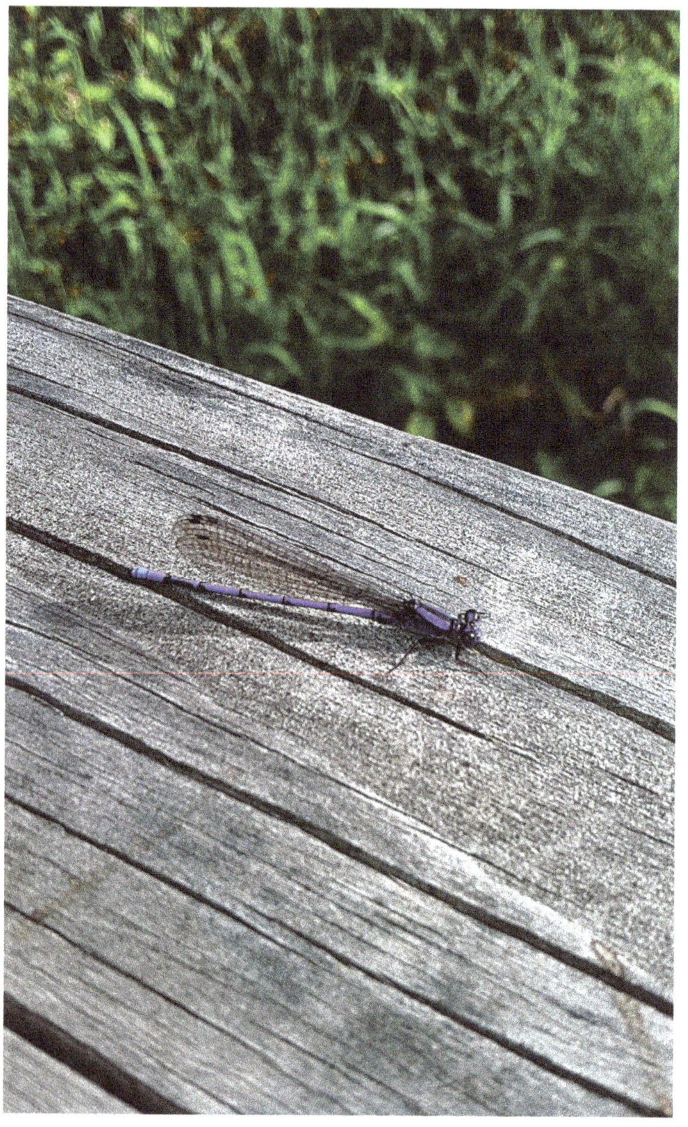

:: OCTOBER

Sitting with Dragonflies
For Maddie

On Saturday, a friend posted the following on his Facebook page: "Tired today. Plan on doing NOTHING!"

Two hours later, a new post appeared:

"OK, so 'nothing' didn't last long…kitchen is cleaned top to bottom and I'm on my 2nd load of laundry and off to clean the bedroom and bathroom…always something."

There IS always SOMETHING, isn't there?

At a women's group last week, we were asked to think about what we would do—what our hearts most wanted—if we could choose anything, with no regard for obligations, cost, or time. Something "just for us."

"I'd take a month off," I said. "And spend the time just doing nothing."

And then I elaborated: "You know, clean the house, read some books, do some writing, go for long walks, organize the art room, finish a collage, get out in the garden, have friends over for dinner, move the furniture...."

Now, if I had not been the first one to respond, I—like the other women in the room—may have had time to think of something a little sexier:

Travel to Paris.
Learn a new language.
Finish my novel.
Drive cross-country.
Overcome fear.
Lose 15 pounds.

But none of these—my interesting-as-a-cardboard-box list or the yummy-sexy-life list—can remotely be considered "nothing."

Just this past weekend, I was in Massachusetts with the intent to do nothing but visit with friends and relax. As is always the case when I go away, I brought my trusty backpack, filled with all sorts of nothing—the short story to edit, the book to read, the unfinished journal entry, the art supplies—just in case.

Just in case, what?

Just in case I end up doing nothing?

So, what is "doing nothing" anyway? Are there different interpretations—can there be? Is one woman's nothing another person's tyrannical To Do list? Are we genetically predisposed to different levels of nothing?

A magical woman I knew named Maddie used to talk of sitting outside and letting dragonflies dance in her hands. "I can hear their wings flutter," she whispered once, as if sharing a secret.

The secret is this...nothing is not nothing.

Doing nothing is simply the freedom and time and space to do something. To do those somethings that ground us, that help us rebalance, that bring us joy. Cleaning the house? Maybe. Or reading a good book. Going for a walk in the woods. Or simply sitting with dragonflies.

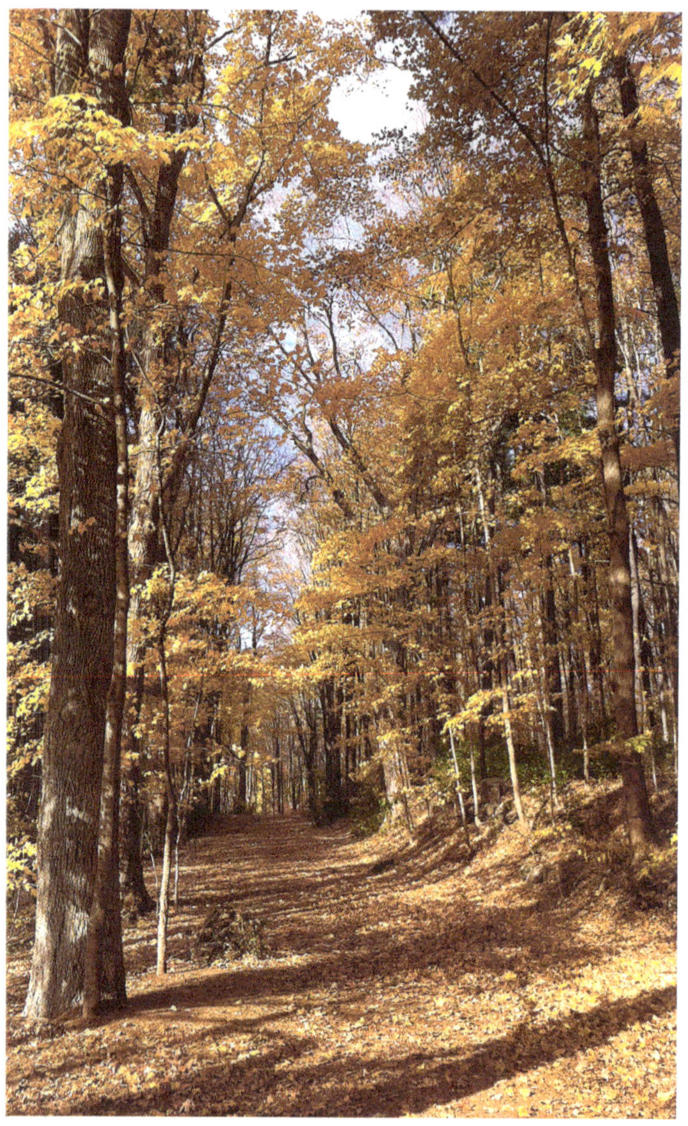

We're Walking

"Everybody needs beauty as well as bread, places to play in and pray in, where Nature may heal and cheer and give strength to body and soul."

— John Muir, "The Hetch-Hetchy Valley"[18]

Small Reminders

On Sunday, while walking along one of my favorite paths, I spotted a familiar shape, though it took a moment to register: praying mantis. Gently and without hesitation, I held out my hand and she gracefully accepted the transport from heavily-trod trail to the safe refuge of a sugar maple's trunk.

These chance encounters with Earth's creatures give me a chance to pause. To consider: why was this set down in my path? What am I to learn from this?

In Kalahari tradition, "Mantis" was a Bushman, according to Ted Andrews' *Animal Speak: The Spiritual & Magical Powers of Creatures Great and Small*.[19] Like fables, "there are abundant tales that speak of Mantis and his adventures.... Whenever Mantis got himself into trouble, he would go off and hide. He would then go to sleep and dream a solution to his problem."

"This epitomizes the keynote for this insect—the power of stillness," Andrews explains. "Through learning to still the outer mind and go within, we can draw upon greater power—physical, emotional, mental, or spiritual. That stillness can be simple contemplation, a meditation, or even sleep and dreams."

Andrews continues on to say: "We can learn to use the stillness in varying degrees—whether for creativity or for healing—and this is part of what the praying mantis teaches."

How is it that I stopped along the path on Sunday? Stopped at that specific spot?

How is it that I saw the praying mantis, so perfectly camouflaged in the fall leaves?

And how is it that I could quickly recognize the perils of a busy path for it and not for myself?

"When we pay attention to and acknowledge a nature totem," writes Andrews, "we are honoring the essence that lies behind it. We are opening up and attuning to that essence. We can then use it to understand our own life circumstances more clearly. We can share in its powers or 'medicine.' Nature totems…are symbolic of specific kinds of energy we are manifesting and aligning with in our life. The animal becomes a symbol of a specific force of the invisible, spiritual realm."[20]

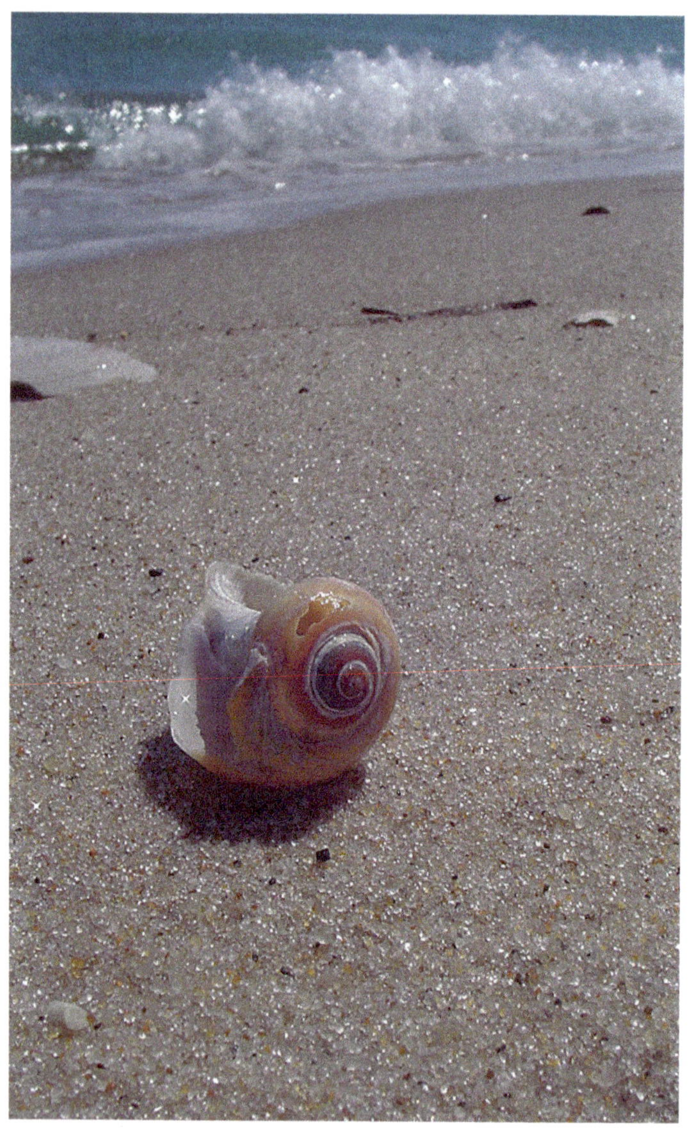

Gift from the Sea

In her treasure of a book *Gift from the Sea*, Anne Morrow Lindbergh uses the analogy of shell collecting to reflect on the beauty of patience and the value of simplicity. She encourages open hearts, insisting that if we open ourselves to Nature, our souls will find its great abundance.

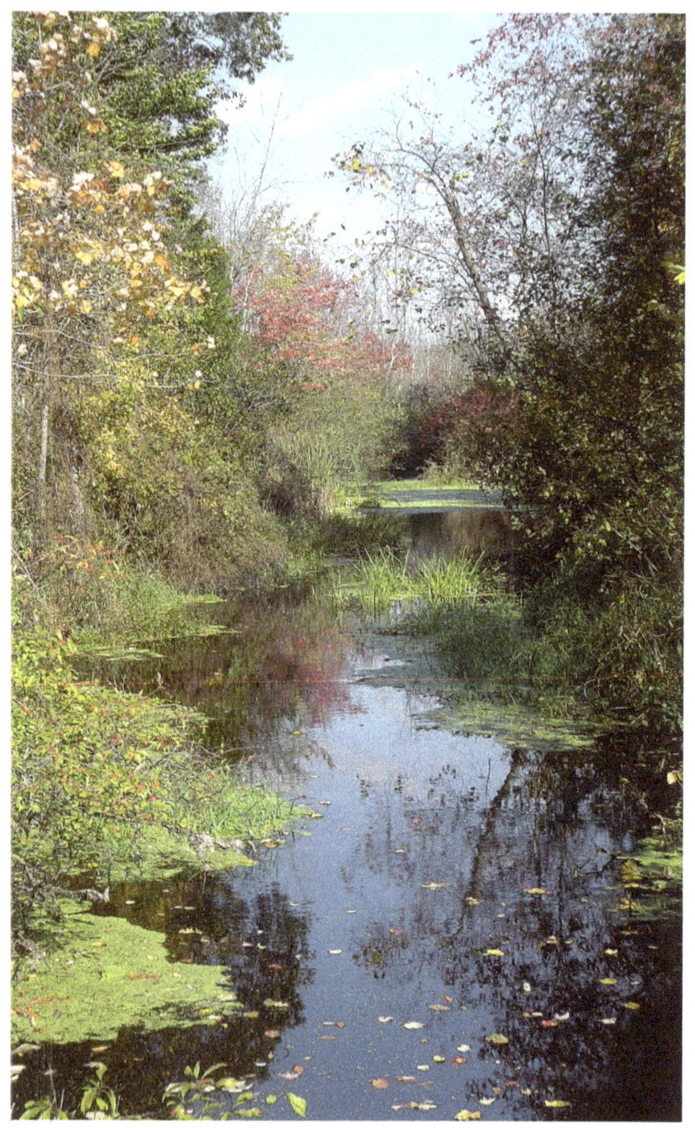

:: NOVEMBER

Quiet Mirrors

"Only in quiet waters
things mirror themselves
undistortedly.

Only in a quiet mind
is there adequate perception
of the world."

— Hans Margolius, *Values of Life: Essays and Notes*[21]

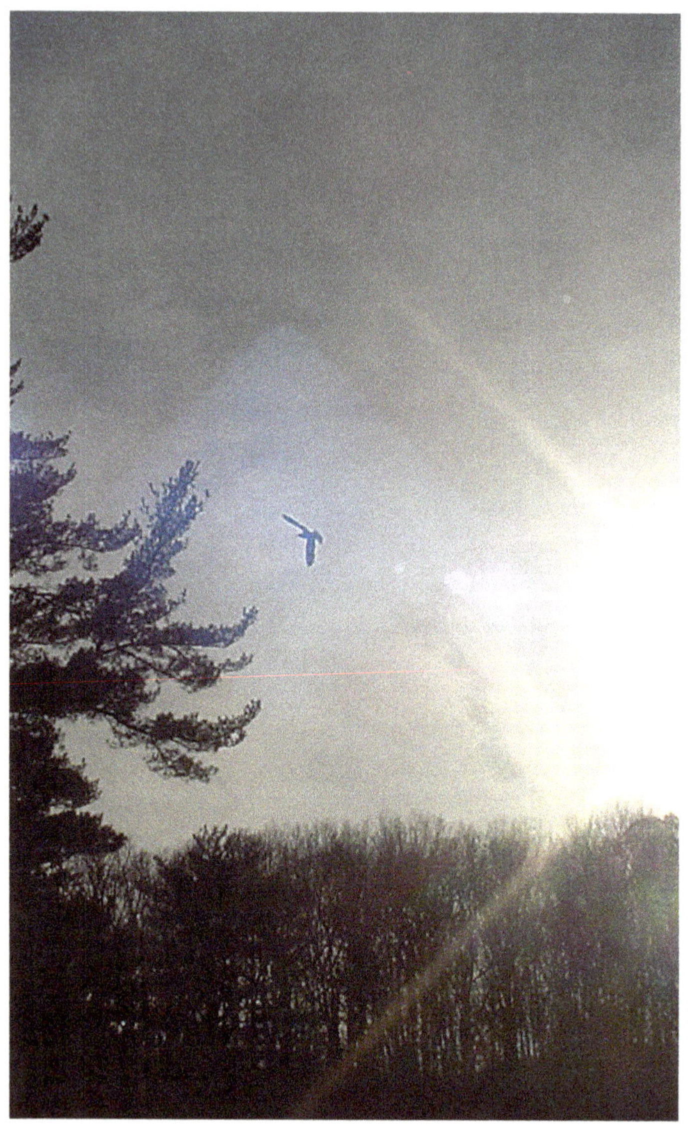

:: DECEMBER

When Magic Has Its Say

Clearing my head this day is like clearing a thicket of brambles and branches.

My thoughts have attached themselves to me like burrs, and it is too cold to stop and try to pull them off. So we walk along the frozen path together.

It is quiet in the woods now.

Except for the still-suspended leaves that rattle from branches.

Except for the shuffle of birds and squirrels, like last-minute shoppers.

Except for the chatter in my head.

I drown out the distraction with words. Words upon words that will become the paragraphs of a new blog post, a new poem, a new something written with thoughts…

about

chance

and fate

and the random nature of Nature

and chaos

and order

and control

and...

Watch! Watch!

The blue jays are screeching. Loud and shrill calls echo in the trees along the path.

Watch! Watch!

So alarming in tone even I stop to look. Is it a cat? A fox? And then I see it. Way up high in the crook of a pine tree—a barred owl.

There I am, tangled up with thoughts about chaos versus order...and in swoops magic!

*In cultures worldwide, the owl is a symbol of wisdom,
power, intuition, mystery, protection, messages and
change. Birds, in general, are often thought of as
mediators between the material and spiritual worlds and
owls in particular are seen in this light. Owl energy has
a peaceful and protective vibration and as "rulers of the
night" they teach us to acknowledge our shadow selves.
The owl invites you to peer into the dark as they can and
they give you courage to accept and come to love all that
you find there.*

— Waking Planet[22]

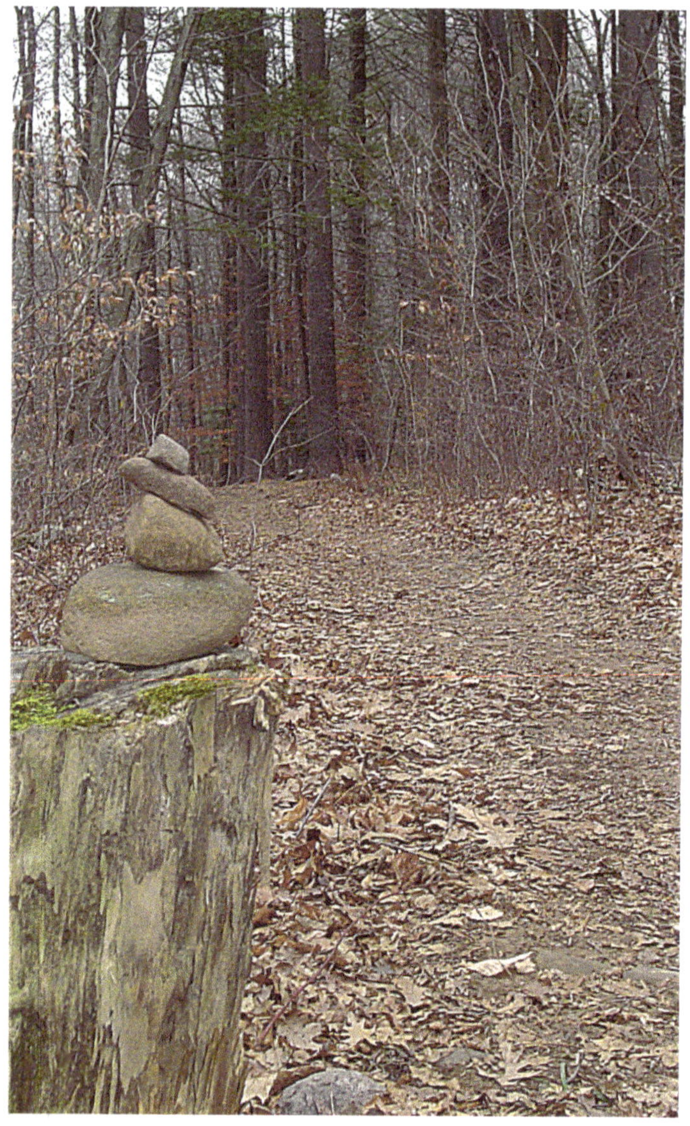

What Faeries Be?

What faeries be,

What winter elves,

do play amongst these trees?

What magic acts

are set about

to trick us with such ease?

What spell was cast

upon these rocks

to make them playful so?

What trickery?

what wizardry?

Perhaps we'll never know.

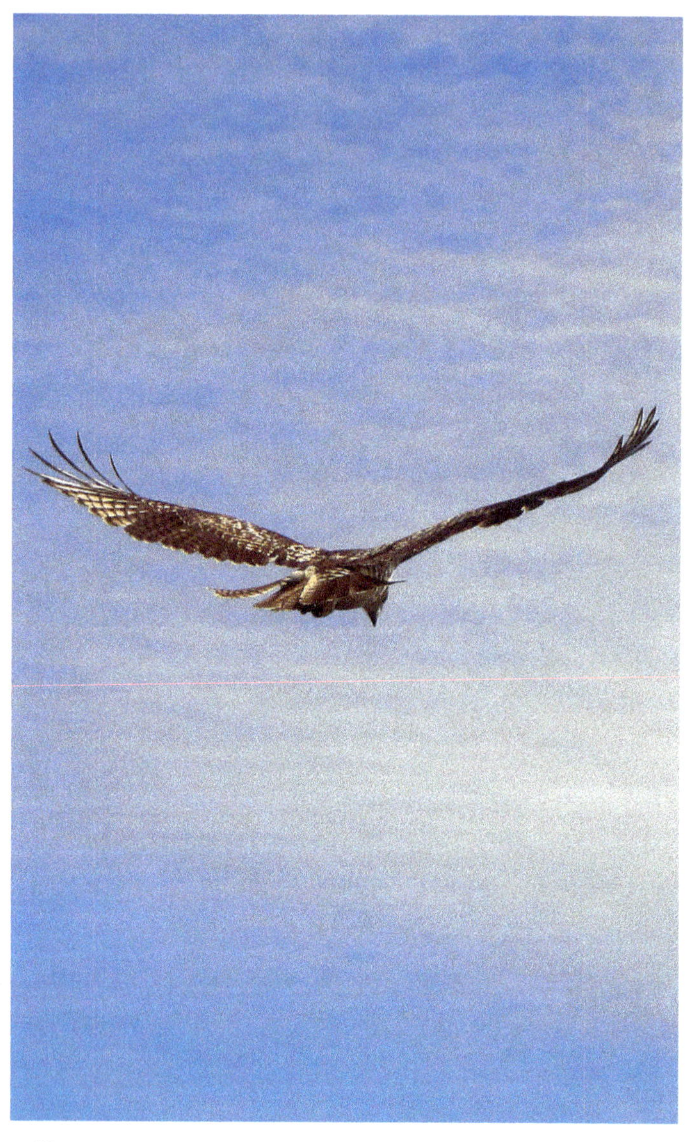

:: JANUARY

At the Right Time

I don't really believe in coincidences. Things happen for a reason," a friend emailed this week. "What that reason is I am not sure.

But I have faith. For example...our friendship. You and I have not met by chance. It was set up deliberately. All of the stars aligned and here we are emailing and talking about BIG things."

We *were* talking about BIG things: God and faith things.

"Breathe," she writes. "It will all be okay."

"Have faith," she is trying to tell me. I know.

But it's the "faith" part I've been struggling with lately.

You know that feeling, I am sure. When everything is good and smooth and easy, it is likewise easy to have faith.

JUVENILE RED-TAILED HAWK

But when things get a little bumpy—faith is harder to keep steady, harder to hold.

I was thinking on all of this the other day as I was driving through town—coincidence, friendship, faith—when I saw a rainbow in the sky.

It was a giant, circle rainbow that went full around the late afternoon sun. As I followed it with my eyes, I saw a hawk perched on a tree nearby. Just that second, it flew across the road, up and over a roadside billboard, and into the woods.

I watched it soar off, and then my eyes came to rest back on the billboard. There, in giant, can't-miss letters:

CELEBRATE LIFE

Hawk "is the messenger bird," writes Ted Andrews in *Animal Speak: The Spiritual & Magical Powers of Creatures Great and Small*. "Whenever it shows up, pay attention. There is a message coming."[23]

"I don't really believe in coincidences. Things happen for a reason," my friend emailed this week...

Postscript: My To Do list today included heading back across town to get a picture of the billboard. The list read: Bank, Post Office, cat food, *Celebrate Life*.

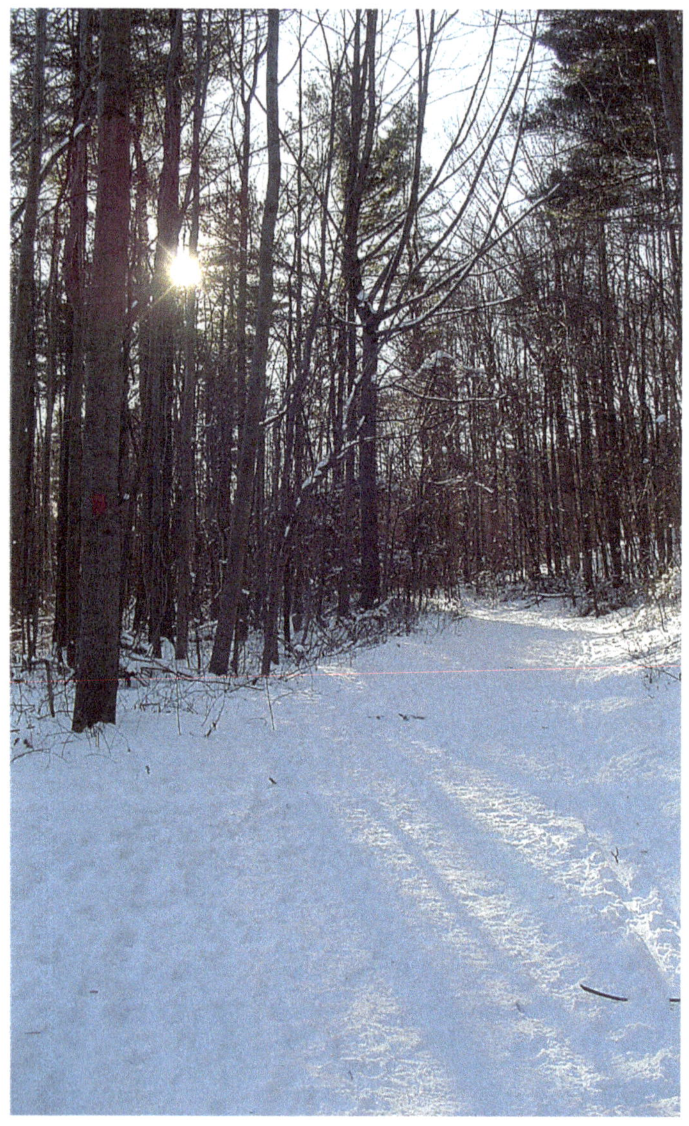

Happiness Follows

"All that we are is the result of what we have thought: it is founded on our thoughts, it is made up of our thoughts. If a man speaks or acts with a pure thought, happiness follows him, like a shadow that never leaves him."

— *The Dhammapada*[24]

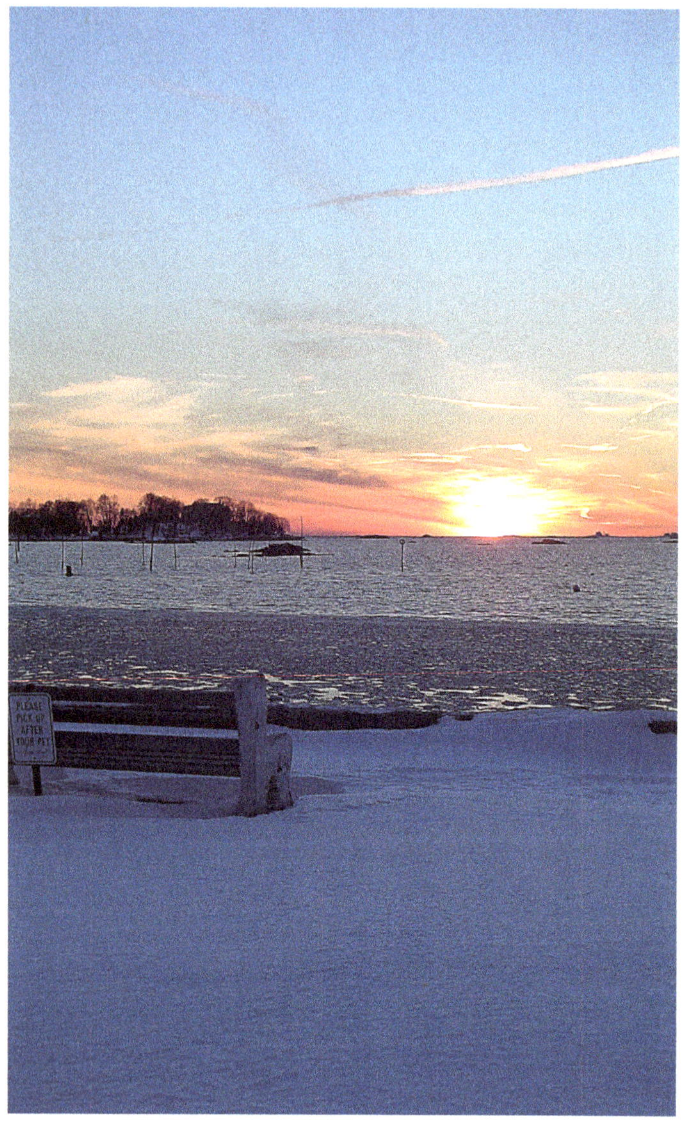

PLEASE
PICK UP
AFTER
YOUR PET

:: FEBRUARY

Sunday in the Park

"And I learned what is obvious to a child. That life is simply a collection of little lives, each lived one day at a time. That each day should be spent finding beauty in flowers and poetry and talking to animals. That a day spent with dreaming and sunsets and refreshing breezes cannot be bettered."

— Nicholas Sparks, *The Notebook*[25]

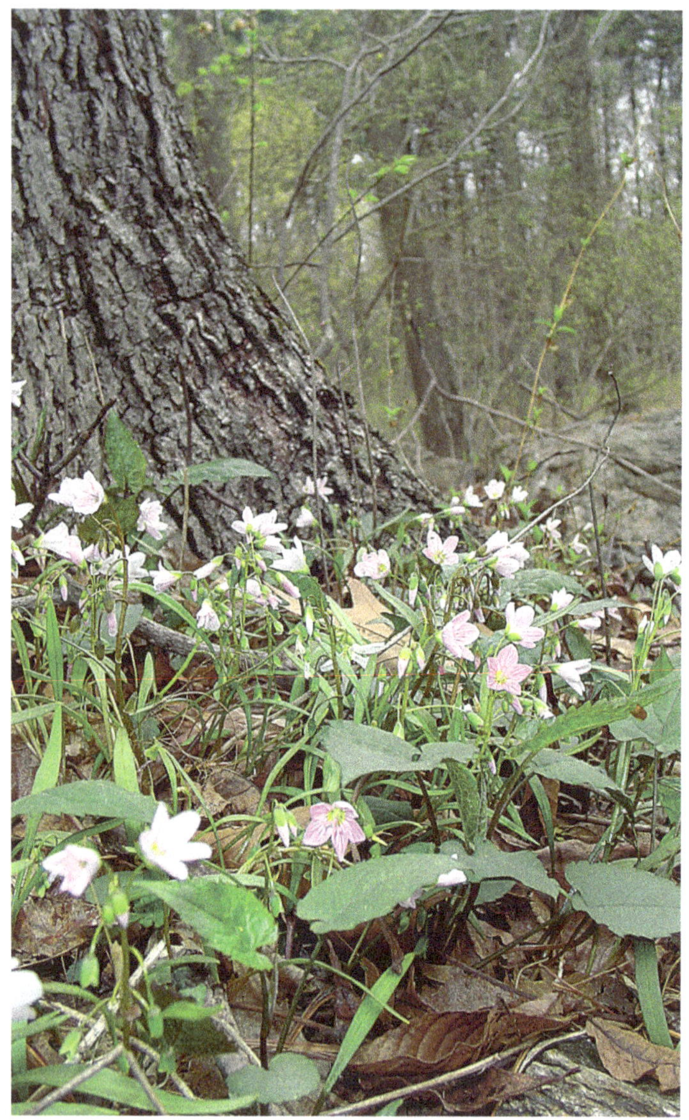

:: MARCH

Happy Flowers

"Look at the trees, look at the birds, look at the clouds, look
at the stars...and if you have eyes you will be able to see that
the whole existence is joyful. Everything is simply happy.
Trees are happy for no reason; they are not going to become
prime ministers or presidents and they are not going to
become rich and they will never have any bank balance. Look
at the flowers—for no reason. It is simply unbelievable how
happy flowers are."

— Osho, *Love, Freedom, Aloneness:*
   The Koan of Relationships[26]

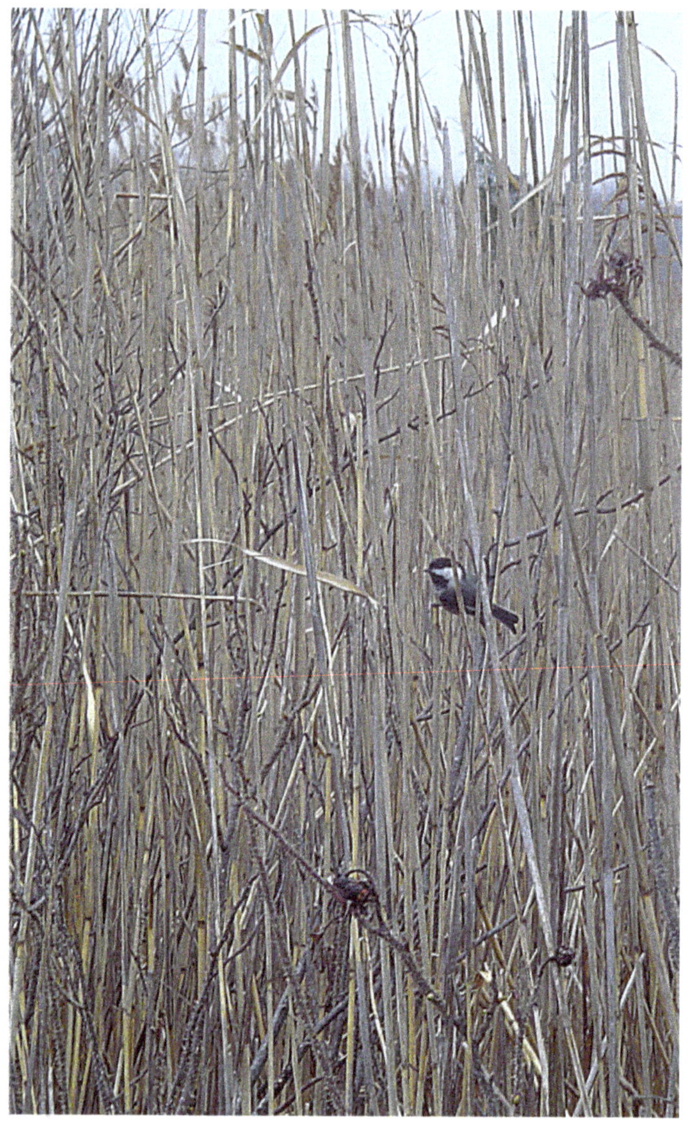

:: APRIL

Nothing to Debate

I t's beautiful no matter what, isn't it?" the woman spoke
quietly as she and her old springer spaniel passed me on
the trolley bridge.

She caught me snapping photos of the harbor in the
middle of a late afternoon drizzle. The scene looked to be
painted entirely of Payne's Gray and Antwerp Blue—a pale
watercolor landscape washed by this early spring rain.

"It IS beautiful," I smiled back at her in agreement.

We do this. This woman and I who pass each other often
at this part of the trail. She and I and the many others who
have the chance to walk this hallowed path along the shore.
No matter who we are or what we believe, we do this:

"It's beautiful, isn't it?"

"What a wonderful day to be here!"

"It's just amazing!"

"Aren't we lucky?"

The funny thing is, we say this all the time. On gorgeous sunny days, when the marsh is teeming with life. In the bitter cold of winter, when the silence drapes around us like a blanket. And on days like this, when it seems wiser to be inside than out—it's beautiful here.

But I hadn't come to the trail to talk about beauty. I'd come to write my rebuttal.

The night before, I stumbled on some emailed words that caught in my gut—parochial words presented in an uncompromising (and joyful) manner. They were those arrogant kinds of words that proliferate ignorance and hate.

My anger wouldn't leave me—it churned all day. I thought a walk would help me find my own words to right the wrong, change the mind, convince and persuade.

"As if I have the correct answer?" I mocked myself.

And then an egret took flight across the marsh. And all around me, there were signs of the divine blessing that is this place. The ospreys that danced in courtship last week sat patiently on a new nest. Two cormorants bobbed and weaved in the shallow waters of low tide. A field mouse hopscotched puddles in the moss.

And slowly I forgot. The passion of the debate fell away like the rain dripping off the ancient rockface, down lichen into the damp leaves below.

"Do you know?" I laughed at the chickadee who stopped when I called to it.

"Do you know who made this place?"

"You are closer to God than I, surely you have the answer?"

It laughed and took flight, as I looked to the sky and thanked God, Universe, Allah, Brahma, Vishnu, Shiva, Pangu, and the Great Spirit. It's beautiful...no matter who is responsible.

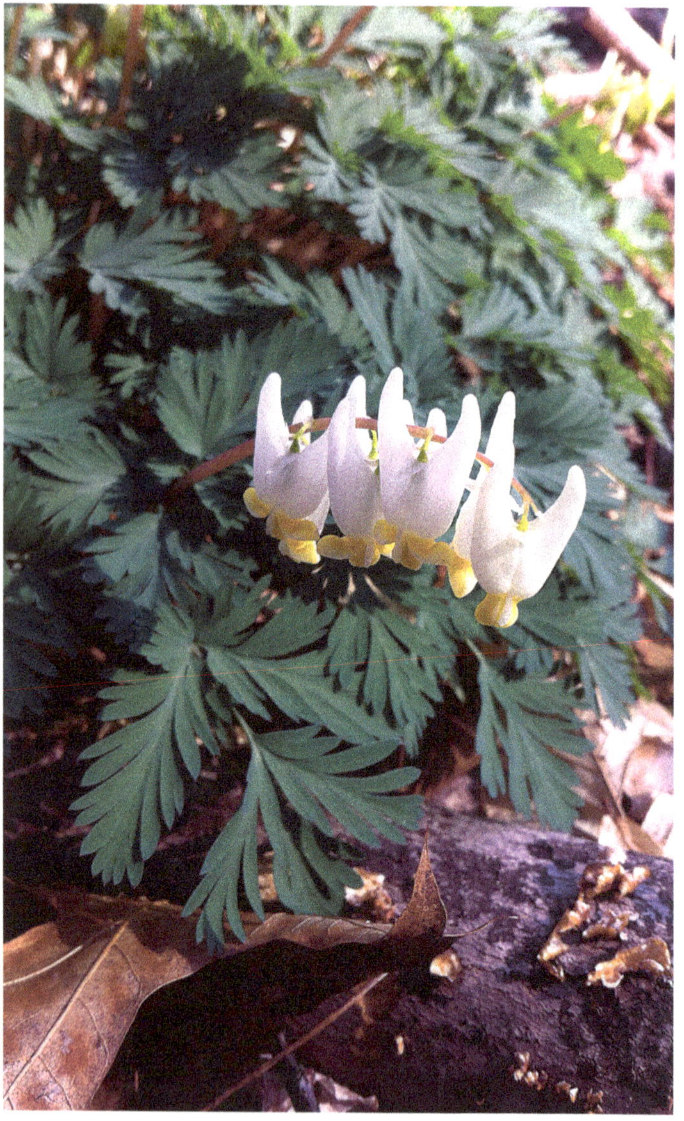

With Eyes Cast Down

"In silence, oneness with
everything is possible...."

— Dale Carlson, *Stop the Pain: Adult Meditations*[27]

My mind was busy as I walked to the trail. It was one of those days. Should I go left? Should I go right?

I am always indecisive when my mind is occupied otherwise.

On this day, I went right—instead of left—and found my way along a narrow, woodland path.

DUTCHMAN'S BREECHES

Up a hill. Across a small, spring stream. Into the quiet of the woods—I was breathing again.

There, in front of me, a patch of new ferns congregated along the edge of the trail, and I paused for a moment.

Down on one knee, I snapped a few photos and realized in that very action, I had stopped worrying about the worries that were worrying me. Funny how that happens, isn't it?

"It turns out meditation is not separate from daily life," writes Dale Carlson in *Stop the Pain*. "It is taking time for walking or sitting in silence so your life can be reflected in the pool of that silence."[28]

Right there, I gave myself an assignment:

Look down, be quiet, pay attention.

And there they were. Small clusters of wildflowers, patches of delicate ferns, bright colors, and playful shapes. New spring life, all along my path.

I never would have seen them.

Look down, be quiet, pay attention.

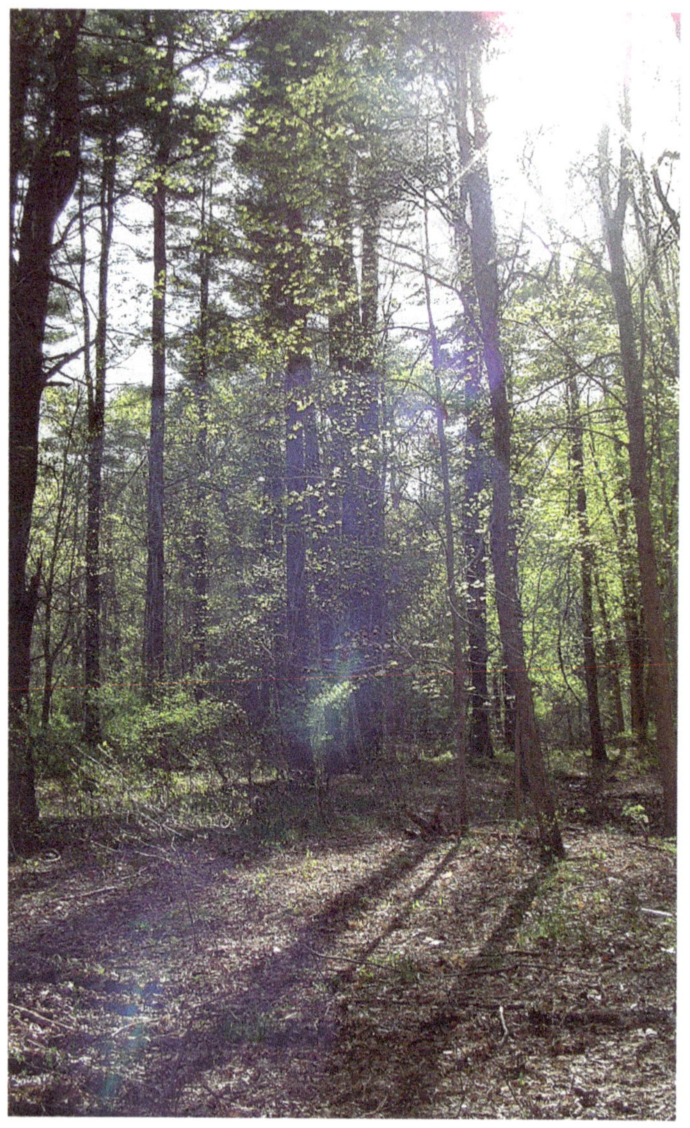

:: MAY

Spirit Woods

I talk with you often,

as I walk along these paths.

Quiet words meant for paper soon

are a slow-paced conversation

through the grove of stately pines

and gathering of birch by the pond.

I tell you tales of men

who built great walls of stone,

of winged creatures who

sing from treetops

and call out from the mist,

of striped-backed scouts who

cheep our arrival in the hollow.

There is a spot in these spirit woods

where I think I would show to you

the royal stag upon the hill,

the princes of Rohan

in full gallop through the glen,

the ethereal Viviane

in wait for Arthur.

Perhaps you would think me mad,

talking to myself and

set in wait like this for myth.

And then, as sure as I am of love,

you would see it too.

That spirit of magic

as she shows herself here for you.

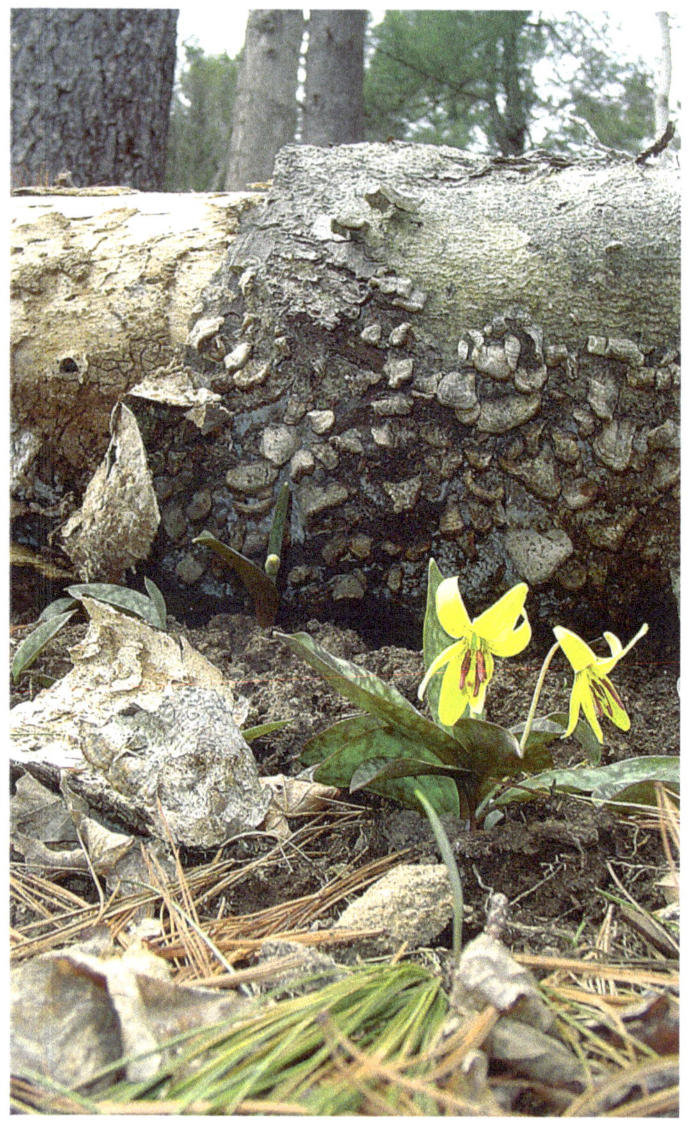

To Be Thrilled

"To find the universal elements enough; to find the air and the water exhilarating; to be refreshed by a morning walk or an evening saunter; to find a quest of wild berries more satisfying than a gift of tropic fruit; to be thrilled by the stars at night; to be elated over a bird's nest, or over a wild flower in spring—these are some of the rewards of the simple life."

— John Burroughs, *Leaf and Tendril*[29]

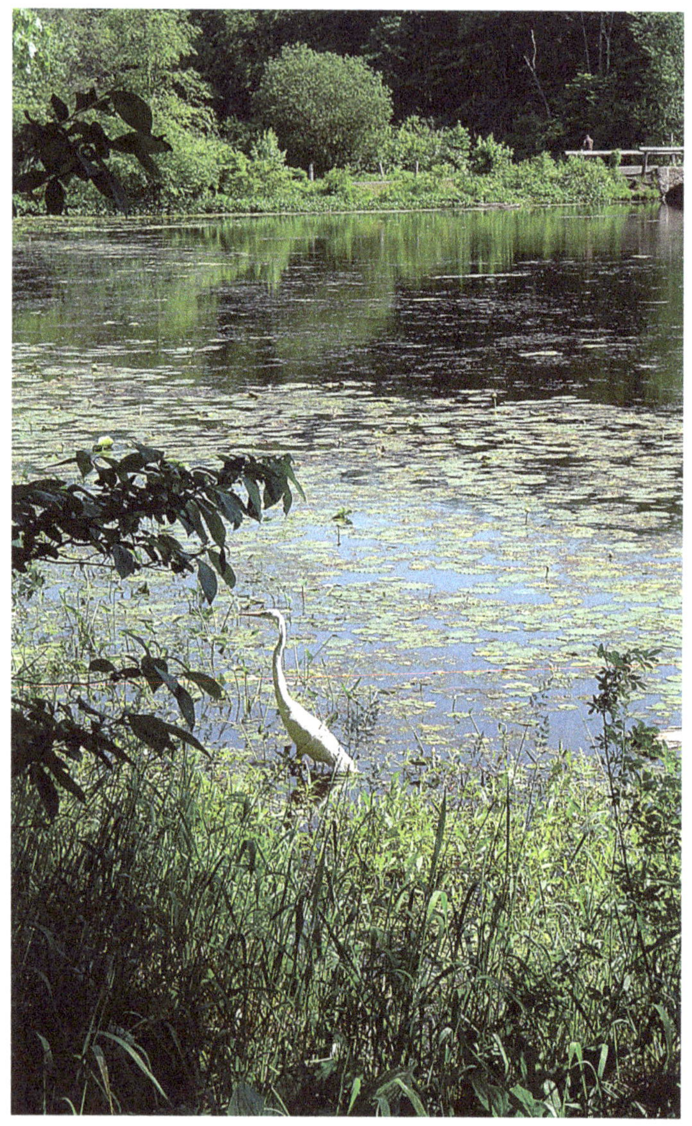

:: JUNE

On a Day's Walk

"But in every walk with Nature one receives far more than he seeks."

— John Muir, *Steep Trails*[30]

GREAT EGRET

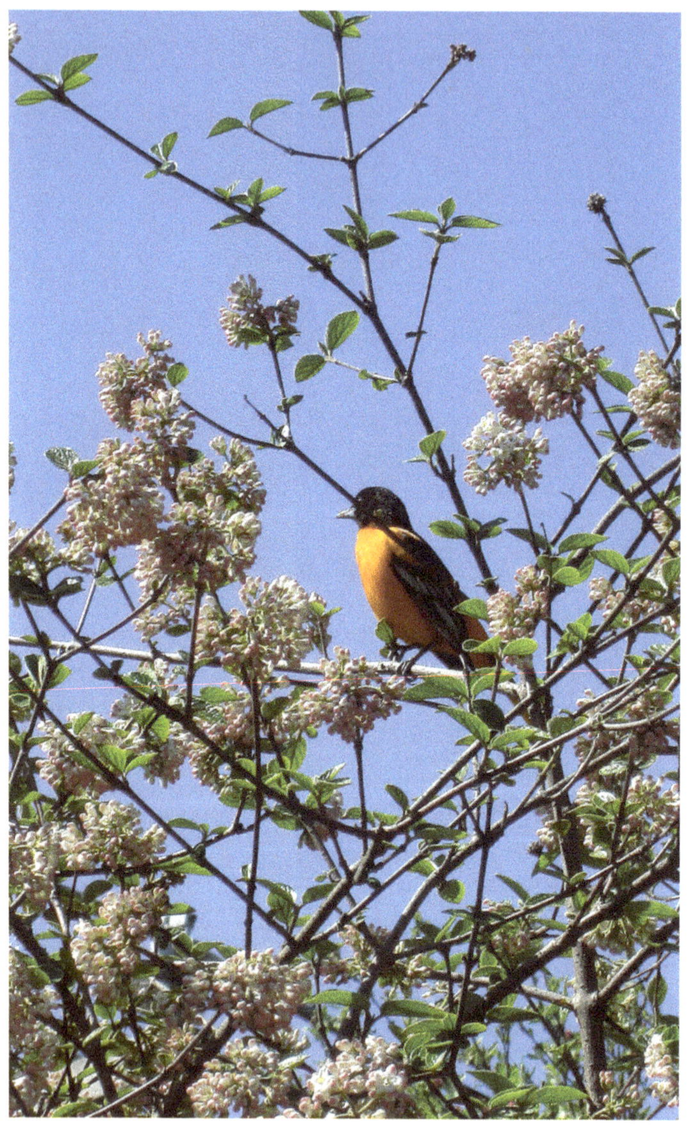

Take a Moment?

"A bird does not sing

because it has an answer.

It sings because

it has a song."

— Chinese Proverb

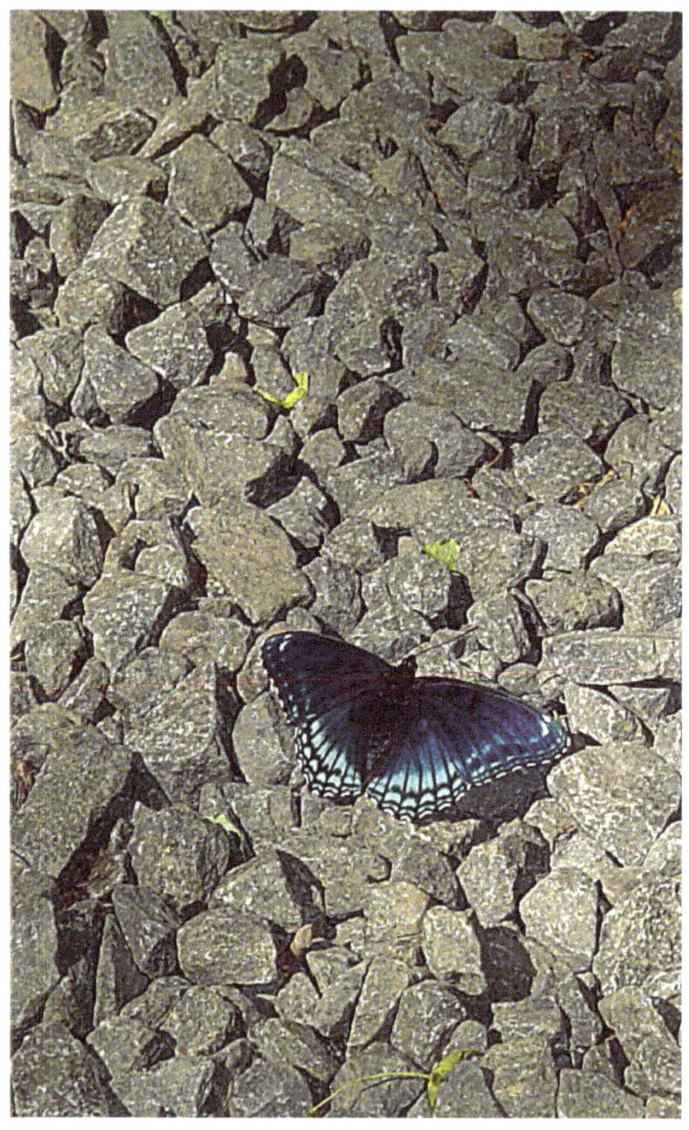

:: JULY

Butterfly Sitting Softly

"Happiness is like a butterfly.

The more you chase it, the more it will elude you.

But if you turn your attention to other things,

It comes and softly sits on your shoulder."

— L. Richard Lessor[31]

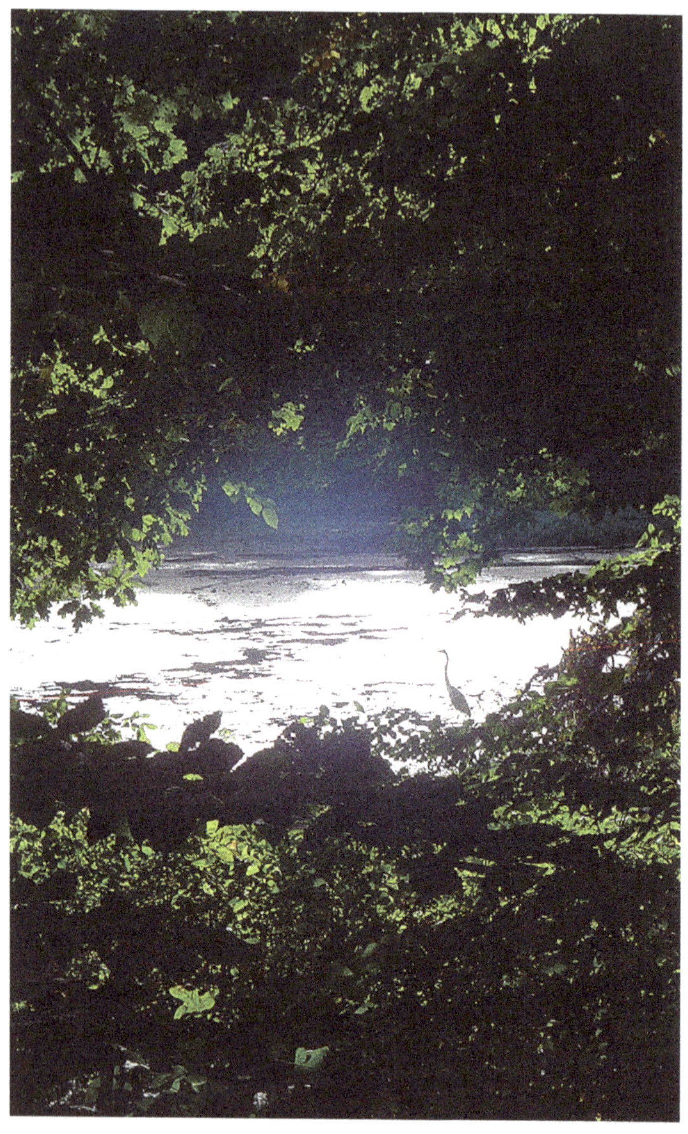

I Have Something to Show You...

There are moments when the Universe quietly whispers, "Come here, I have something to show you." She did it just the other day and showed me this. Thought I would pass it along...

DESIDERATA
by Max Ehrmann

Go placidly amid the noise and the haste,
and remember what peace there may be in silence.

As far as possible, without surrender,
be on good terms with all persons.
Speak your truth quietly and clearly;

and listen to others,
even to the dull and the ignorant;
they too have their story.

Avoid loud and aggressive persons;
they are vexatious to the spirit.

If you compare yourself with others,
you may become vain or bitter,
for always there will be greater and lesser persons
    than yourself.
Enjoy your achievements as well as your plans.
Keep interested in your own career however humble;
it is a real possession in the changing fortunes of time.

Exercise caution in your business affairs,
for the world is full of trickery.
But let this not blind you to what virtue there is;
many persons strive for high ideals,
and everywhere life is full of heroism.
Be yourself. Especially do not feign affection.
Neither be cynical about love,
for in the face of all aridity and disenchantment,
it is as perennial as the grass.

Take kindly the counsel of the years,
gracefully surrendering the things of youth.
Nurture strength of spirit to shield you in sudden
    misfortune.

But do not distress yourself with dark imaginings.
Many fears are born of fatigue and loneliness.

Beyond a wholesome discipline,
be gentle with yourself.
You are a child of the universe
no less than the trees and the stars;
you have a right to be here.
And whether or not it is clear to you,
no doubt the universe is unfolding as it should.

Therefore, be at peace with God,
whatever you conceive Him to be.
And whatever your labors and aspirations,
in the noisy confusion of life,
keep peace in your soul.

With all its sham, drudgery, and broken dreams,
it is still a beautiful world.
Be cheerful. Strive to be happy.[32]

That Which Distracts Us May Not

We were "talking" about enlightenment. It was barely 10:00 a.m., and our talk evolved as pieces of thought shared in a comment field on her blog.[33]

"Are we, every one of us, capable of extraordinary beauty, and wisdom, and kindness—if only we realized it?" asked my friend Judith.

"I believe we are," I replied, "but there are so many distractions between here and 'realized.' I suspect enlightenment needs great expanses of quiet, reflection, and disconnection in order to take root and flourish."

Another friend was talking about Henry David Thoreau and our important and necessary connection with Nature as a source of joy.

The song of a green frog interrupted my thoughts as I read her words, and I glanced up and noticed how the morning sun dappled the grass outside the window. I suspected I had not looked up from the whirring computer since the yard was shadowed in last night's darkness.

This is not the disconnection to which I was referring.

Twenty minutes later, I was in the woods, walking a path I had not explored since summer set upon us with its mid-July ferocity. When I left the house, I imagined immediate connection—to pick where we left off in June, with quiet observation and reflection. But there were bugs. Lots of bugs.

I have visited with the metaphor of these bugs before—as pesky as my thoughts, as persistent as my worries, as distracting as life's other interruptions that follow us. With the incessant buzzing about my head, how would I ever find that cherished space and quiet I was seeking?

"Fine," I said out loud, in surrender to the swarm of gnats. So I paid attention instead to the rhythm of my swatting—two hands at first in a ballet above my head, then alternating hands to rest each for a while.

I walked this way for close to an hour—hands as windmills around me, through a pine forest, into a sunny meadow, and up to the clearing where the woodpecker sings. At the footbridge, I watched two dragonflies dance, then walked carefully up the rocky slope, down to where the stream crosses the path. I walked fast, in that way we do when we have a goal to obtain. All the while swatting with noble attempts to ignore the...damn...bugs?

Where were the bugs? Suddenly, they were gone.

I stopped and breathed deeply to slow my pace. My arms rested at my sides, and I could feel a hint of coolness about my body. The path was quiet—except for a faint call of a warbler off in the distance. Just then, a wide band of sunlight pushed its way though the tree cover and lit up the forest around me until it sparkled, and I wept.

"I think perhaps rooting and flourishing happens in cherishing the significant flash," my friend responded on her blog. "In short—once my long blindness lifts, SEEING simply follows."

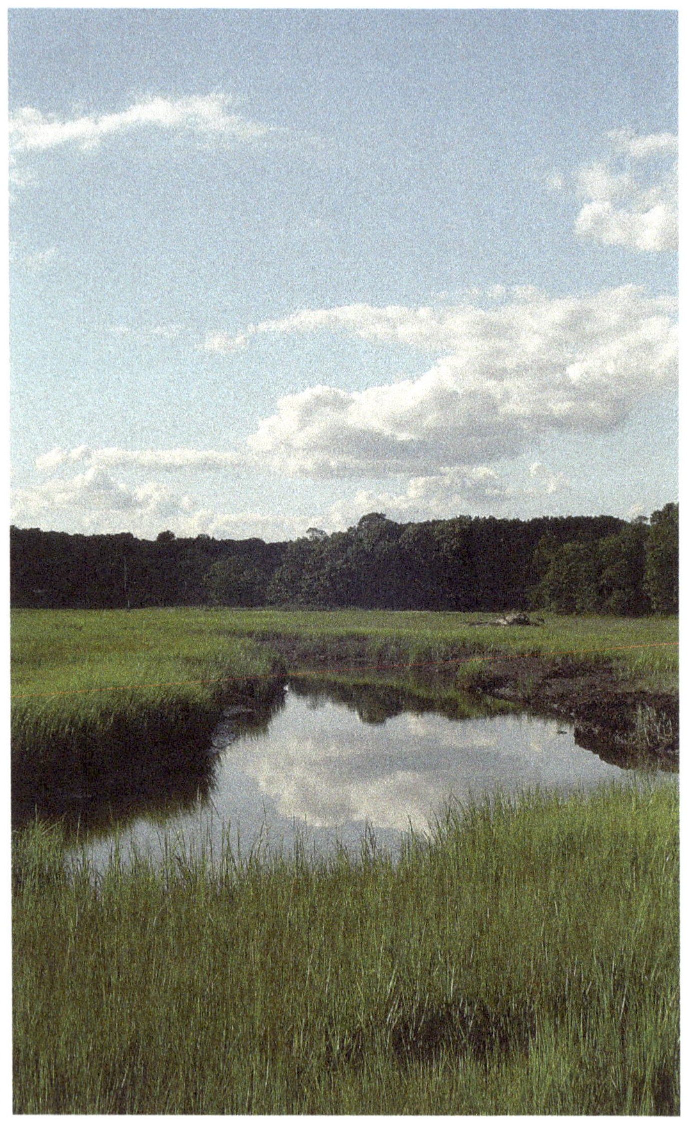

A Short Excursion

"Fresh beauty opens one's eyes wherever it is really seen,
but the very abundance and completeness of the common
beauty that besets our steps prevents its being absorbed
and appreciated. It is a good thing, therefore, to make short
excursions now and then to the bottom of the sea among
dulse and coral, or up among the clouds on mountaintops,
or in balloons, or even to creep like worms into dark holes
and caverns underground, not only to learn something of
what is going on in those out-of-the-way places, but to see
better what the sun sees on our return to common every-day
beauty."

— John Muir, *The Mountains of California*[34]

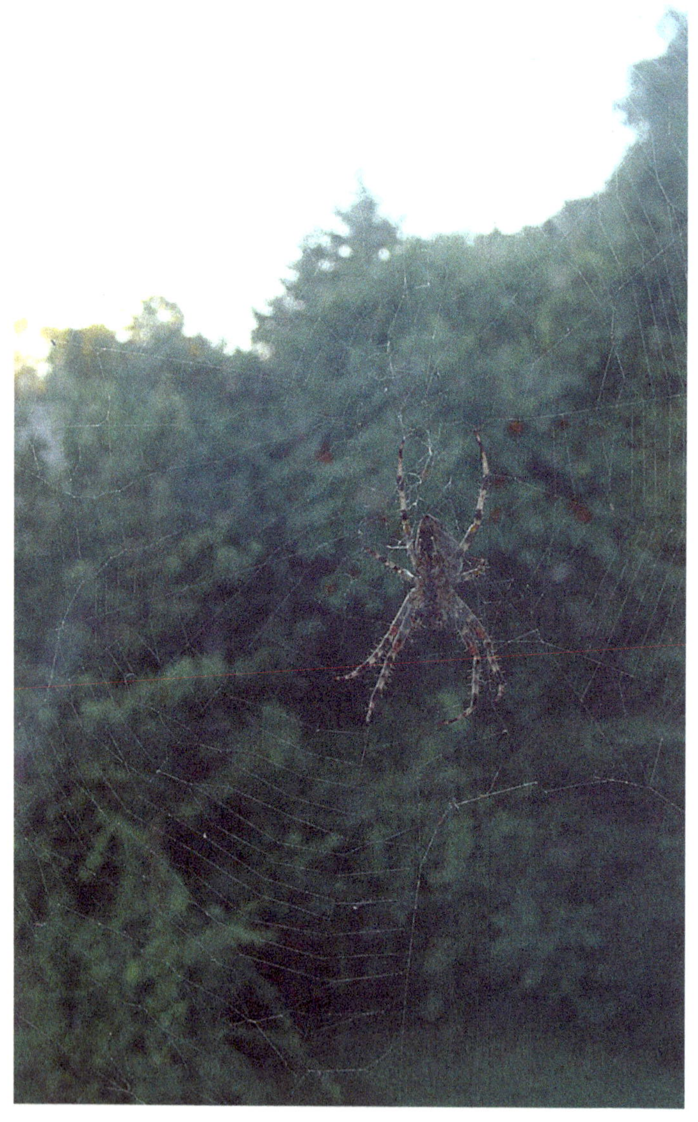

:: SEPTEMBER

She Does Not Play Small, Why Should I?

Orb weaver. Doesn't that conjure up an image of some great goddess weaving planetary trajectories through the paths of comets and falling stars?

She may as well be a goddess, this nimble and beautiful orb weaver spider who has made a home for herself outside my bedroom window. Like Arachne of Greek myth, she weaves her magic in gestures more remarkable than Athena. Each night, offering up the gift of a newly constructed, perfectly elaborate orb-shaped web from which she gets her name.

I've watched her for weeks now, my lovely orb weaver. During the day, she wraps herself into a corner of the window and rests out the sun. As shadows fall, she positions herself in the center of the web and waits with great and unmoving patience. Is she meditating, I wonder, as I pass her on my way to sleep. By morning, she is resting again, a new web sparkling in the morning sun.

This fascination is new for me—this great and unmoving observance of spider. Fear has always gotten in the way. Fear, and a giant wad of paper towels!

But fear has a way of keeping us from things—new discoveries, new adventures, new connections. So, I've been pushing at its boundaries...with spiders. And other things.

"Spider teaches you that everything you now do is weaving what you will encounter in the future," writes Ted Andrews in *Animal Speak: The Spiritual & Magical Powers of Creatures Great and Small.* "Spider reminds us that the world is woven around us. We are the keepers and the writers of our own destiny, weaving it like a web by our thoughts, feelings, and actions."[35]

"Let your light shine," my friend Greg keeps encouraging me. We have been talking about being our authentic selves— being as great as we are, with no excuses.

It's a bigger hat than I'm used to wearing. Like watching spiders—I do it tentatively.

He reminds me of an often-referenced quote by spiritual teacher Marianne Williamson that explains how fear gets in the way of being true to ourselves and our purpose here on Earth. In her book *A Return to Love*, she insists that we are never inadequate, we are only afraid, and if we can let go of that fear, we can manifest great things and inspire others to do the same.[36]

Does that include the fear of spiders, I wonder? Perhaps I will start there.

*If spider has come into your life, ask yourself some
important questions. Are you not weaving your dreams
and imaginings into reality? Are you not using your
creative opportunities? Are you feeling closed in or stuck
as if in a web? Do you need to pay attention to your
balance and where you are walking in life?*

— Ted Andrews, *Animal Speak: The Spiritual & Magical
Powers of Creatures Great and Small*[37]

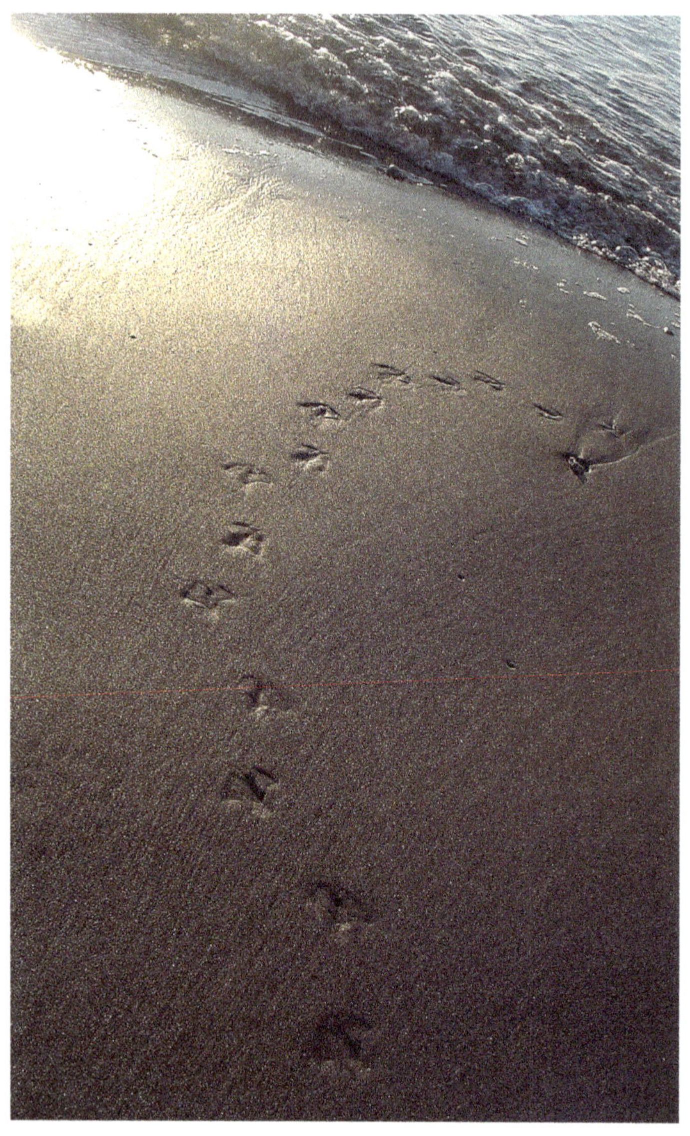

:: OCTOBER

The Calm Before

It was barely past sunrise, too early for the churning of the world to begin. Quiet.

The tide was leaving again. In its wake, small pools sparkled in sunlight like jewels along the shore.

In one I caught a glimpse of heaven—until a soft rush of waves cast ripples and it disappeared at my feet.

Receding water bore channels around islands of sand, where gulls and willets danced in some excited morning ceremony.

A cormorant practiced ancient rituals on a rock surrounded by surf and seemed to feel as blessed as me.

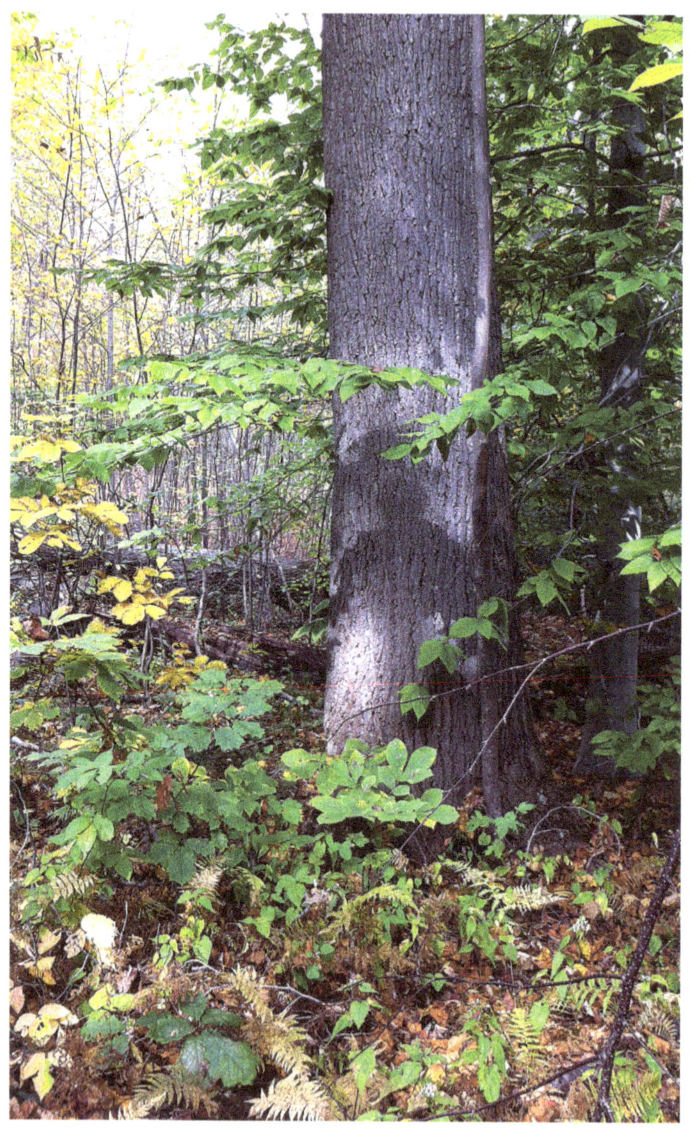

Every Tree Is Full of Angels

If we allow it, we can see holiness all
around us. Magic, even.

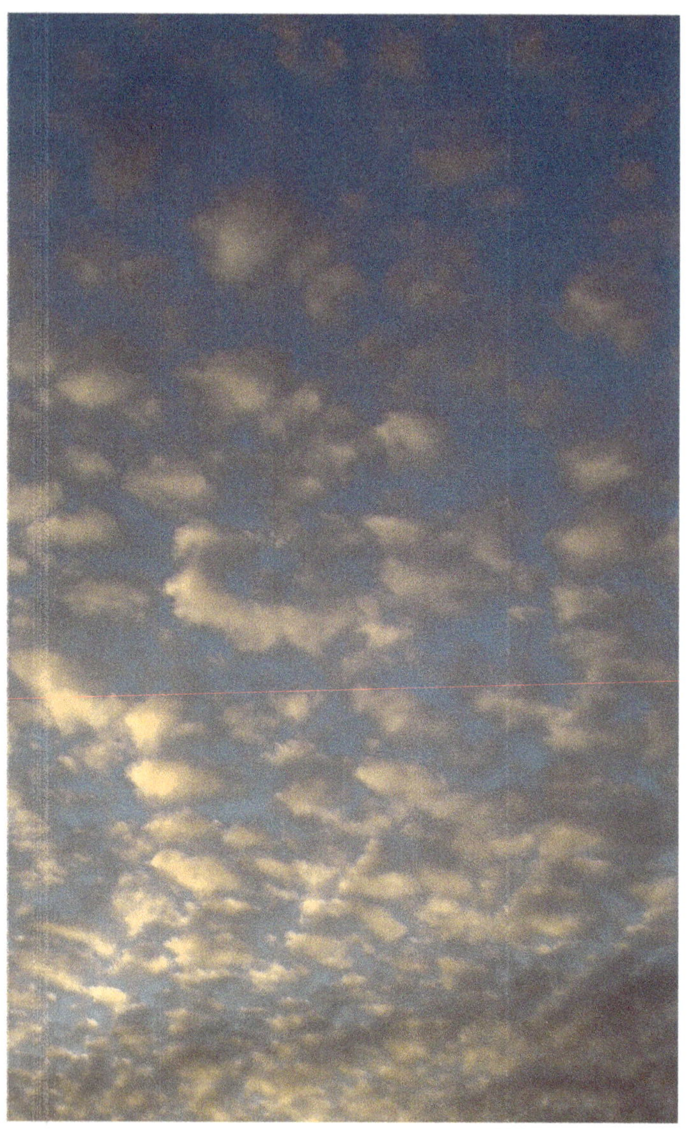

Resistance

There is resistance this morning. I can feel it. It has rooted itself in that spot in the middle of my chest—where anxiety and love commingle sometimes.

I'm trying to breathe through it. Let go. Be in the moment. Recognize it as thought that serves no purpose.

But still there is resistance. And worry. And fear.

And then these beautiful words find their way into my sightline, and I think...

I want to unfold.
Let no place in me hold itself closed,
for where I am closed, I am false.

— Rainer Maria Rilke, *Rilke's Book*
of Hours: Love Poems to God[38]

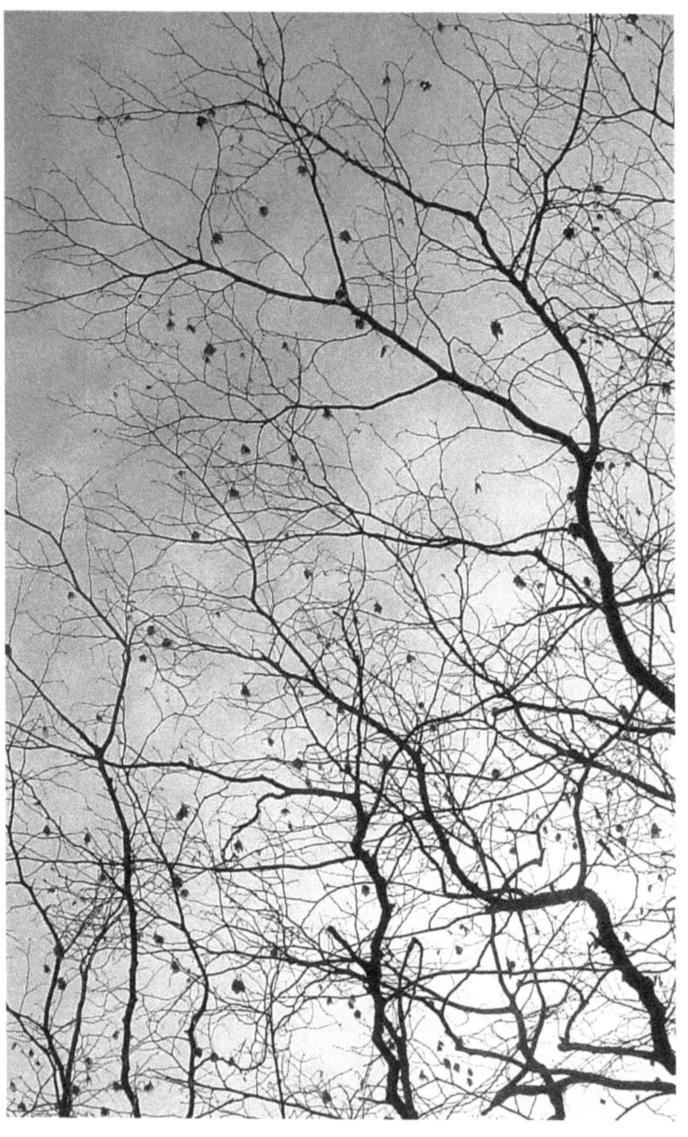

:: NOVEMBER

Pieces of Forgotten

"I felt like lying down by the side of the trail and remembering it all. The woods do that to you, they always look familiar, long lost, like the face of a long-dead relative, like an old dream, like a piece of forgotten song drifting across the water, most of all like golden eternities of past childhood or past manhood and all the living and the dying and the heartbreak that went on a million years ago and the clouds as they pass overhead seem to testify (by their own lonesome familiarity) to this feeling."

— Jack Kerouac, *The Dharma Bums*[39]

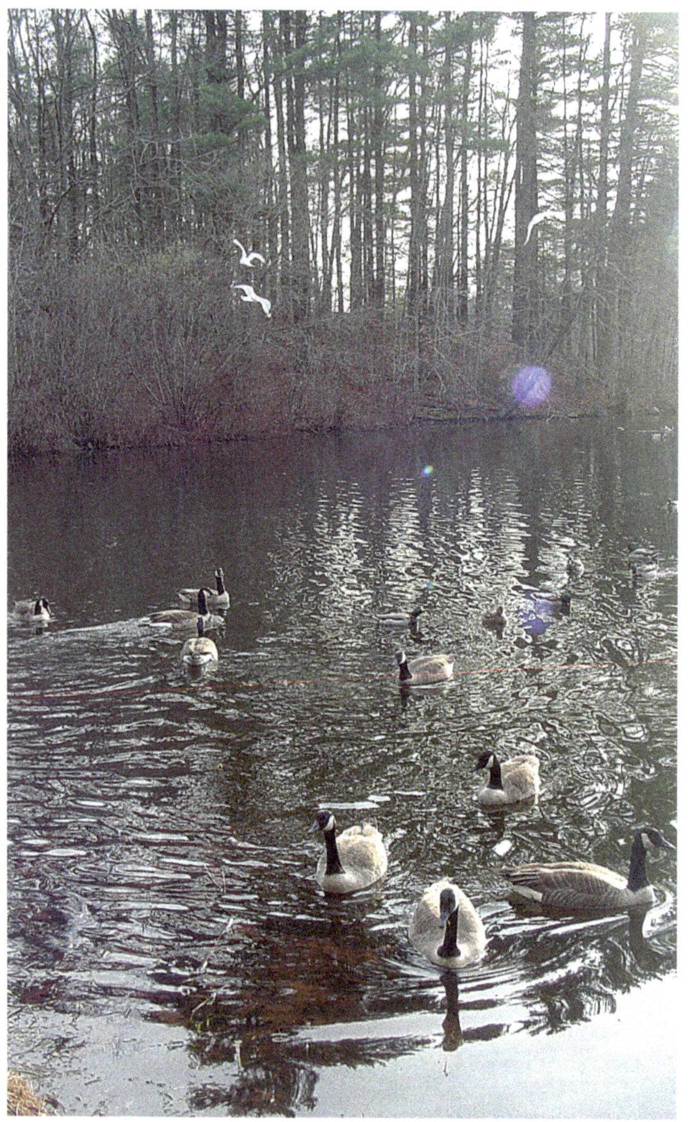

:: DECEMBER

The Geese Aren't Decorating Trees

When I walk in the woods, I understand things. There is a natural rhythm to everything around me—birth, life, death, seasons.

Being in Nature resonates with me—it connects me to this world and this life in a way nothing else does, save for my writing.

And so, when I get stuck, when I don't understand, when I can't glide easily through a situation or a moment—I look to the woods.

I walk. I breathe. I think. I stop thinking. I talk out loud. I laugh.

I move.

And eventually, I find my way out.

Perhaps it is age. Or the velocity of the times we live in. But something has shifted for me.

I am connecting on a different level with this world, and at the same time, I am disconnecting.

The new connection is...amazing. But the disconnect is a little unnerving. It is especially so at this time of year, when the world seems to march like toy soldiers to the beat of the little drummer boy and I...well, I hear "a different drummer."[40]

And so I go walking. Every day.

I see how the trees have shed their finery in exchange for more simple wear. I note the repose of creatures who take this time of year to slow down. I feel the chill in the air—and in my bones—and know it is telling me to slow my own pace as well.

So, I'm taking my cue from the woods this year: simple, quiet, slow.

The experience of Nature is at once personal and universal. It is why there are common threads in our reflections. As companion to this essay, you may want to read the poem "Wild Geese," by Mary Oliver, and explore your own connection to the larger family of things.[41]

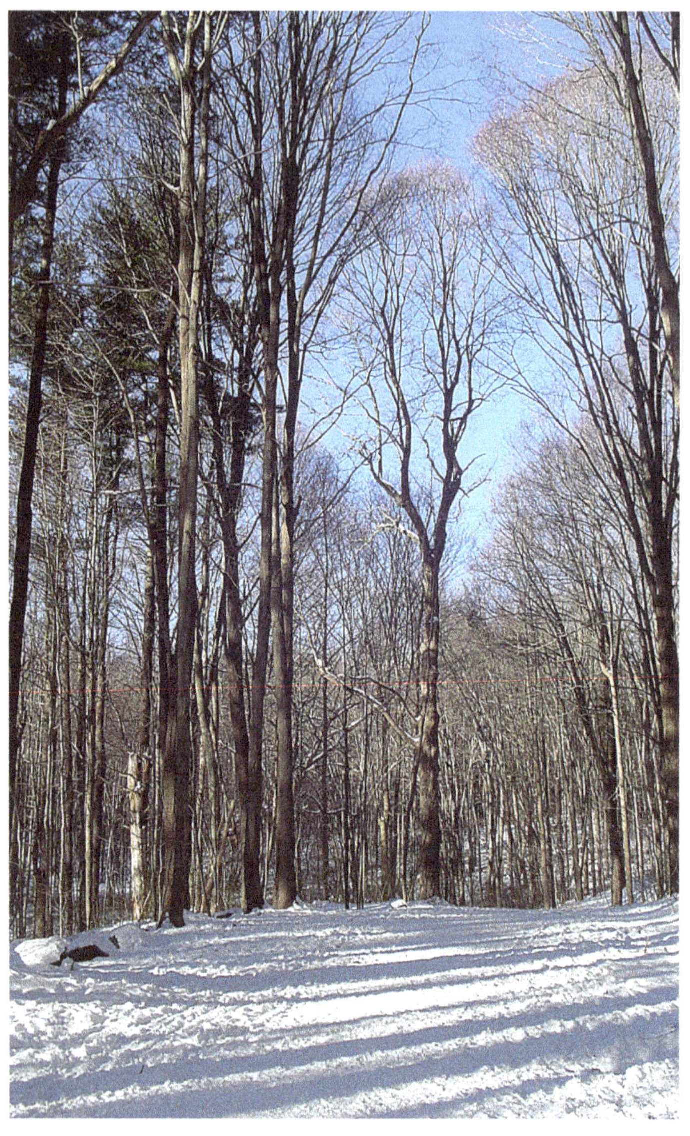

:: JANUARY

Time for a Walk

As soon as the khaki-colored Humvee careened over the side of the cliff and exploded into flames, I knew I needed to get myself out for a walk. I knew it even before I woke up!

My brain—in its Technicolor replay of movies I don't ever let myself watch—was communicating loud and clear. Last night it was exploding Humvees. The night before, Elton John delivered beef tongue from the butcher!

Work and life and houseguests and more work had kept me housebound and away from the woods for too long. And nowhere in that time span had I found a way to let my thoughts rest.

In the woods, they fall from me like raindrops from branches—leaving a little trail behind me as I walk.

The work…

The conversations…

The worries…

"Where have you been?" I asked the woods quietly as I stepped from the trailhead onto the snowy path in front of me.

My hyperventilating breath at the top of the first hill was reminder it had been a while.

So, too, was the deep ache of stretch in my hips as my legs moved back and forth, back and forth.

Slowly, though, it returned. The relax in my shoulders. The strong deep breaths of air. The buzz and hum of movement and thoughts escaping. The quiet.

As I crossed the footbridge and made my way through the tall pine forest where the woodpecker plays hide and seek each summer, I swear I heard a whisper…

"Where have youuuuuuuu been?"

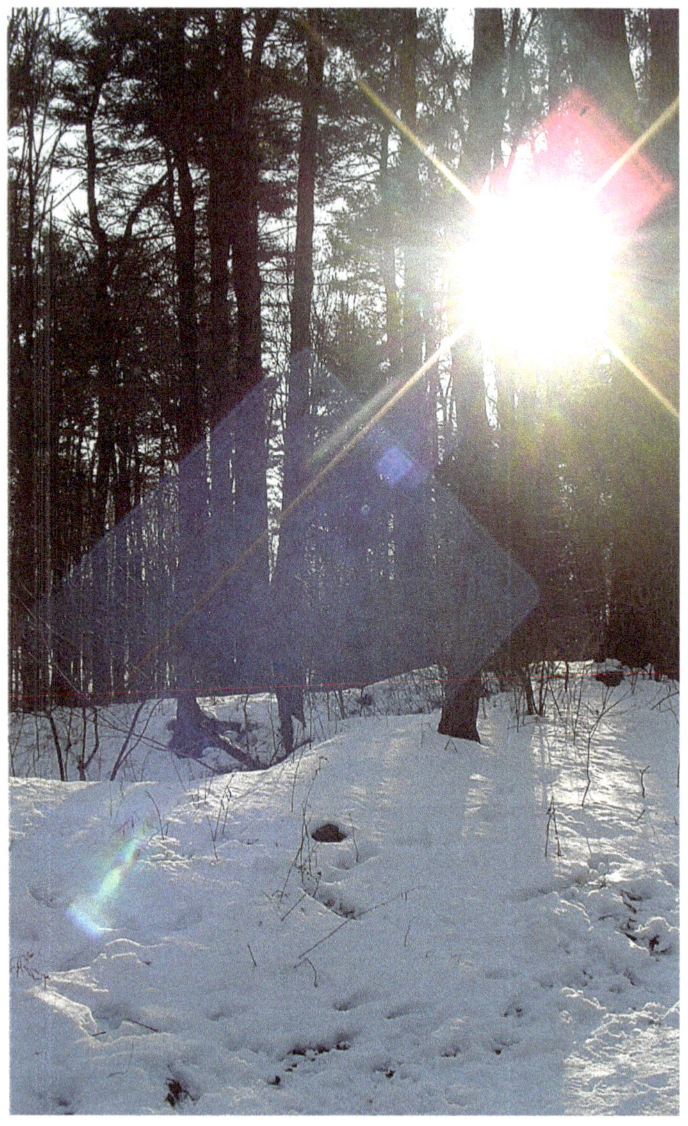

Choosing to Saunter

"There are people who 'hike' through life. They measure life
in terms of money and amusement; they rush along the
trail of life feverishly seeking to make a dollar or gratify an
appetite. How much better to 'saunter' along this trail of life,
to measure it in terms of beauty and love and friendship!
How much finer to take time to know and understand the
men and women along the way, to stop a while and let the
beauty of the sunset possess the soul, to listen to what the
trees are saying and the songs of the birds, and to gather the
fragrant little flowers that bloom all along the trail of life for
those who have eyes to see!"

— Albert W. Palmer, *The Mountain Trail and Its Message*[42]

:: FEBRUARY

Tomorrow and Tomorrow and Tomorrow

Tomorrow I will watch the sun rise. Instead of sitting here infusing my system with more coffee and stiffening my neck at this keyboard, I will put on a hat and coat and scarf and gloves and walk around the corner and watch the sun rise. At 6:30 a.m. was it?—it seems so long ago. It was beautiful, though, the sunrise. Gold and purple and magenta and orange. I sat here watching it from my office window thinking, "I should go watch the sun rise."

I kept thinking that until it had risen and washed out the sky to a pale and overcast gray. The effort required would have taken too much time away from this—this damn machine and this damn work and…and…tomorrow I will watch the sun rise.

Do you think people think the same thing—the day before they die? Or the day before some major life change happens and they can't? Can't watch the sun rise. Can't expect tomorrow.

What does that say about us and our plans and our lists and our dreams? About the things we say we'll do when… when we have time, when we're finished working, when we win the lottery, when we are done.

Why do we just sit here, watching out the window, thinking of the things we'd rather be doing? The things we want to do?

Is that what Nike means? Just do it?

Just have the conversation.
Just make the change.
Just take the chance.
Just let go.
Just love.

Just watch the sun rise.

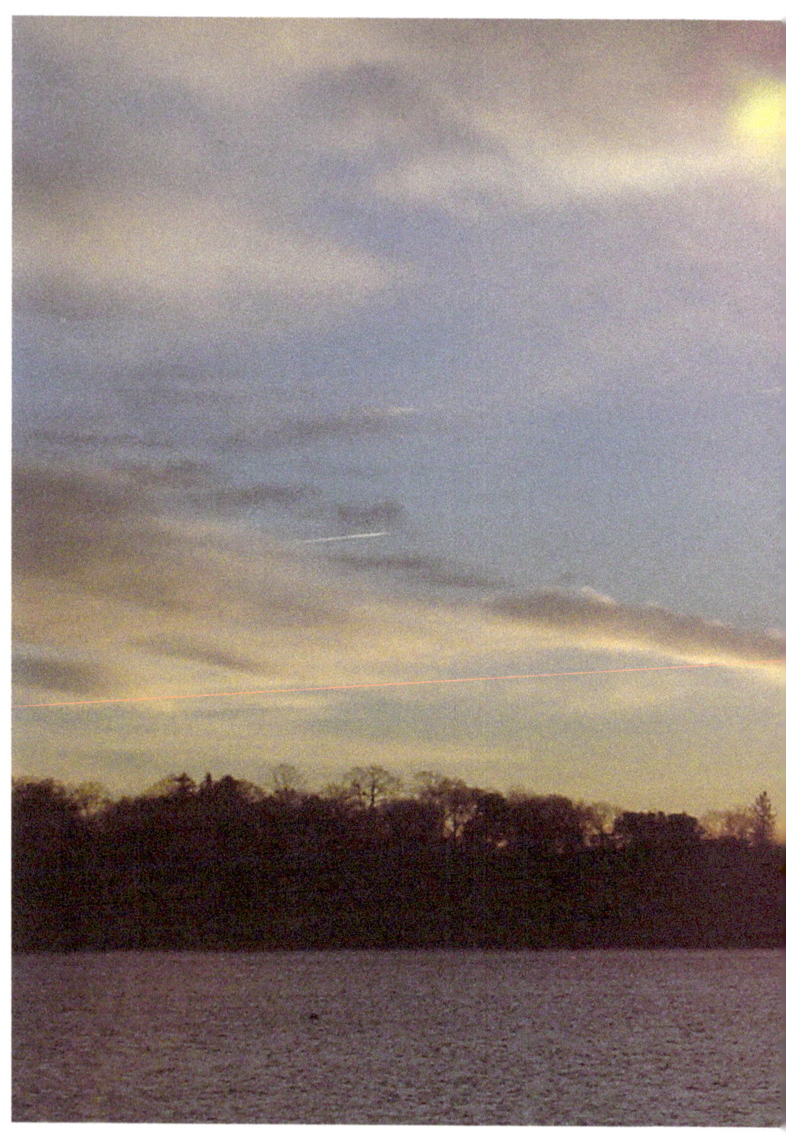

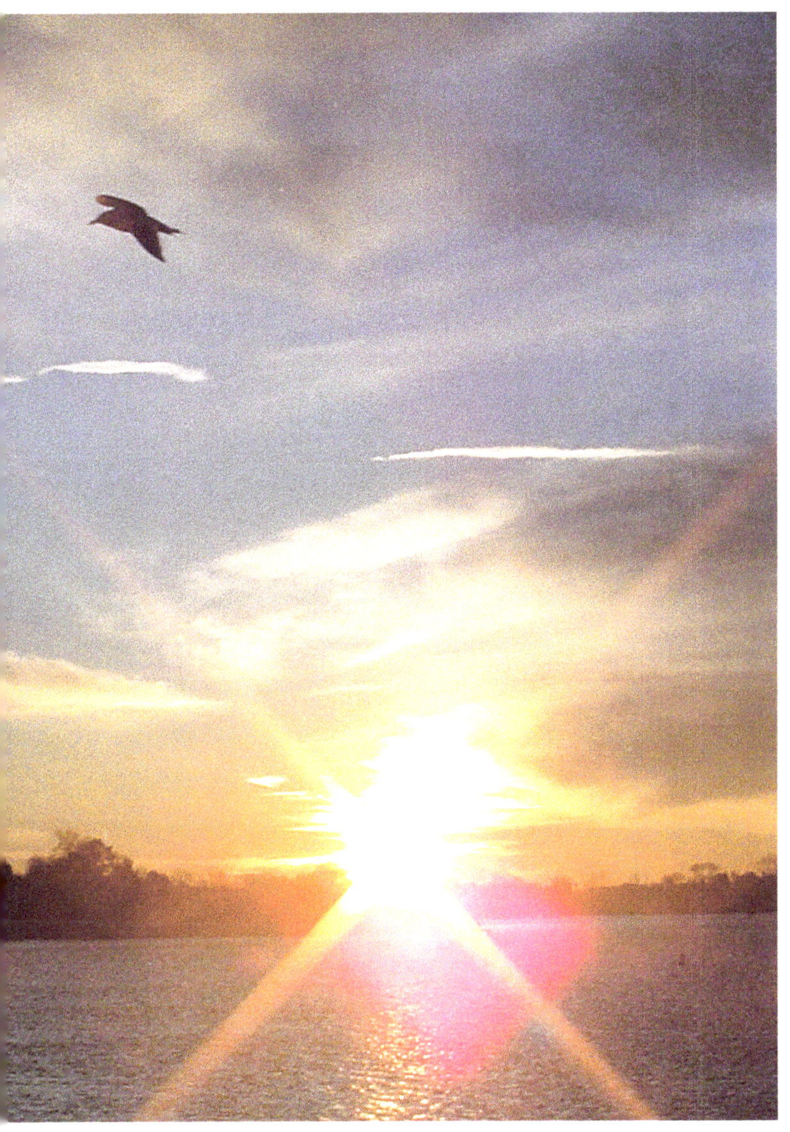

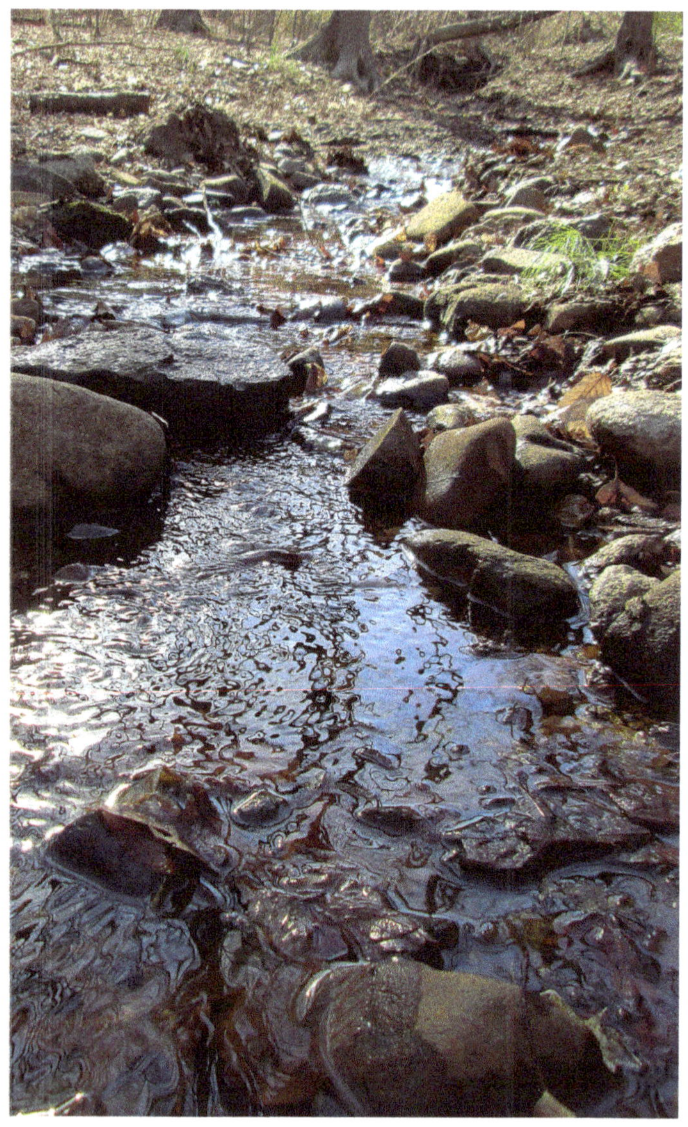

As It Will Go

Several times on my walks recently I passed a dam that wasn't supposed to be there. Unhappy with newly-placed stepping stones, someone chose to create a bridge across the stream that separates the first half of the trail from the second.

Every time I saw it I thought: that's not right, it's going to change the flow of the stream and make a mess.

The irony of the observation didn't strike me until yesterday...

I went for a walk yesterday to clear my head. I'd been struggling all day with something and needed clarity.

At the trailhead, I took a deep breath, pulled my hat down around my ears and asked out loud: "Please help me find resolution."

And then I walked.

I tried to make it a quiet walk—pushing the thoughts out of my way to leave room for the answer. But they would have none of that. There were too many—criss-crossing this way and that.

Just as I thought I had found a conclusion, they'd chime in again. Clamoring about something else, in some other direction.

But what happens next?

Be in the moment.

It's not working.

It is what it is.

I tried to calm them with the Serenity Prayer.

God grant me the serenity
to accept the things I cannot change,
Courage to change the things I can,
And wisdom to know the difference.[43]

Like a mantra over and over again until...

But what happens next?

Be in the moment.

It's not working.

It is what it is.

Then I came to the dam, and sure enough, water was building up behind the rocks and overflowing onto the trail.

"You just can't mess with the natural flow of things," I thought.

And there it was. Clear as day.

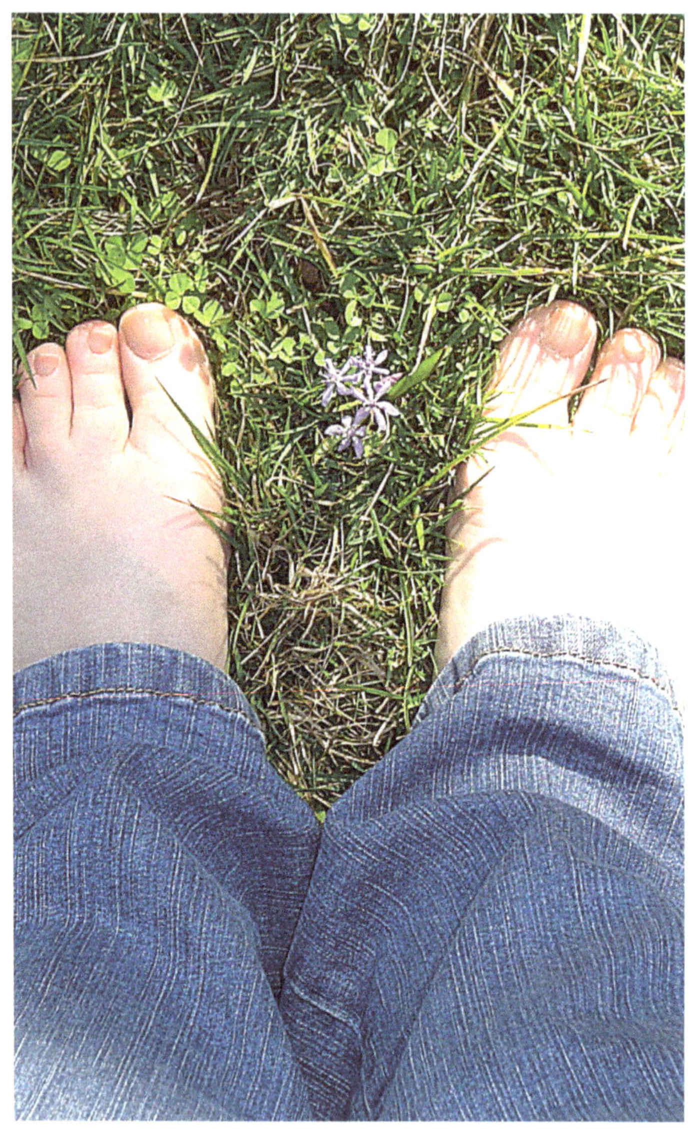

:: MARCH

Present Always

"A single gentle rain makes the grass many shades greener. So our prospects brighten on the influx of better thoughts. We should be blessed if we lived in the present always, and took advantage of every accident that befell us, like the grass which confesses the influence of the slightest dew that falls on it; and did not spend our time in atoning for the neglect of past opportunities, which we call doing our duty. We loiter in winter while it is already spring."

— Henry David Thoreau, *Walden*[44]

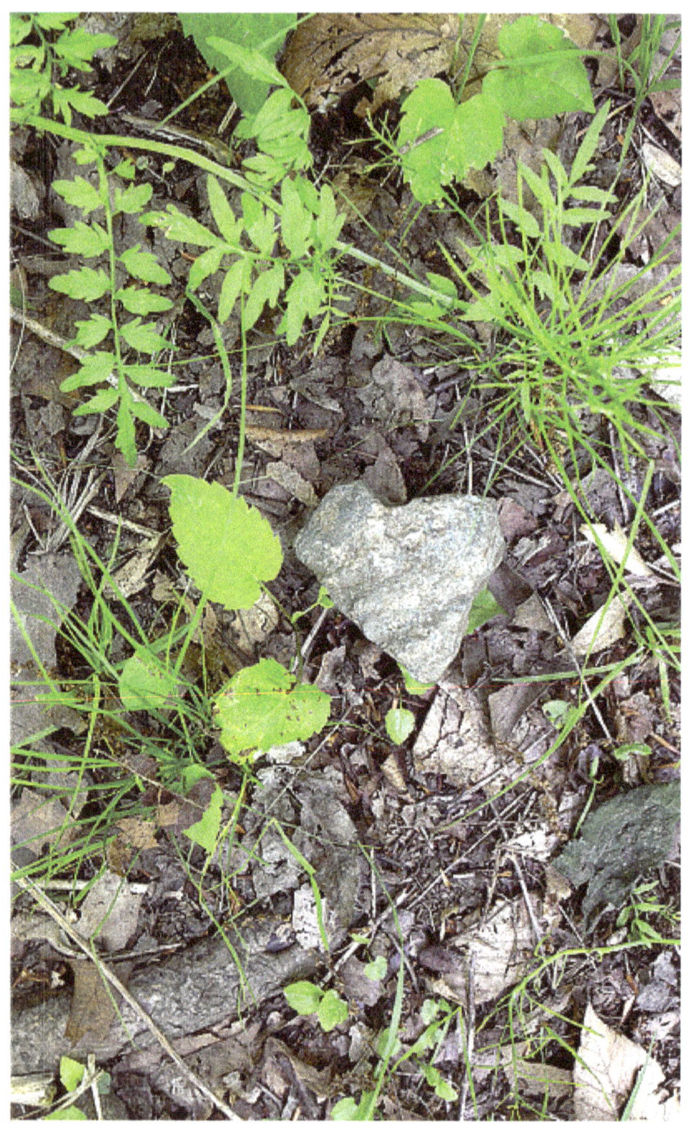

Finding Rocks: A Parable

Lately it seems like every time I look down, I find a heart-shaped rock.

I'm not looking for them. Usually I'm just pausing to catch my breath or take a picture or listen to the woodpecker who has recently returned to the woods. Usually, I'm not paying attention or in focus. Usually, I'm just in joy. And there at my feet is a rock no more or less obvious than the others—except that it's shaped like a heart.

Granted some are a little misshapen. Some require leaps of faith. Some are big and hard to carry. Others are small and vague.

But love is like that.

Sometimes it just shows up, without the need to search.

Sometimes it just shows up, without the need to judge.

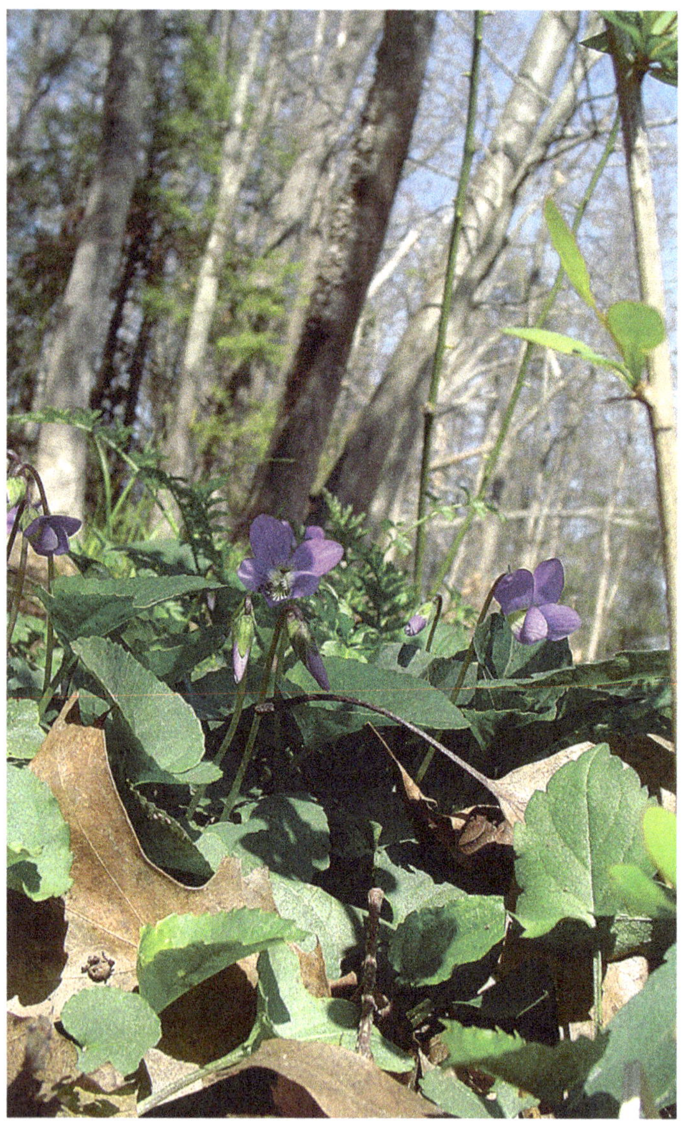

:: APRIL

Being One With

I knew right away it was a magical day in the woods. The gorgeous 50-degree afternoon was accented by a bright blue sky and a soft breeze that sang through the trees.

I saw a trail I'd never seen before, followed it to the edge of the pond and sat for a while. Sat. Quietly. I'd been invited to do so by the turtle who was on the log but disappeared as soon as I sat down. I waited for him to return, but he never did.

So I made my way back down a familiar path until I heard the distinct rustle of a hawk landing in a tree just up a hill. I stood silently for five, maybe ten minutes, watching it perched up high. But, when I decided to get a closer look, he took off into the tops of pine trees nearby. As I continued on my way, he flew above me, casting shadows on the path—he was watching me now, and we both knew it.

A squirrel stopped when I called to her, but dropped her acorn from the startle. "Go ahead, go back and get it," I told her, then stepped gingerly back a few steps to allow safe space. She scurried down the tree, snatched up her meal, then glanced my way as if to say thanks.

A carpenter bee was busily moving about when I came upon her. I watched for a while as she crawled in an out of her burrow—spring cleaning, I wondered?

Walking further and further down the path this way, I could feel peace settle in. If I closed my eyes and breathed, I barely existed—except to feel the breeze on my skin and hear the whisper of trees. My footsteps, my heartbeat, my thoughts were so far away, they sounded hollow and unreal.

From the flirting of birds in the trees to the surprise of late-spring wildflowers come early, the forest was brimming with life and spirit...and suddenly, so was I.

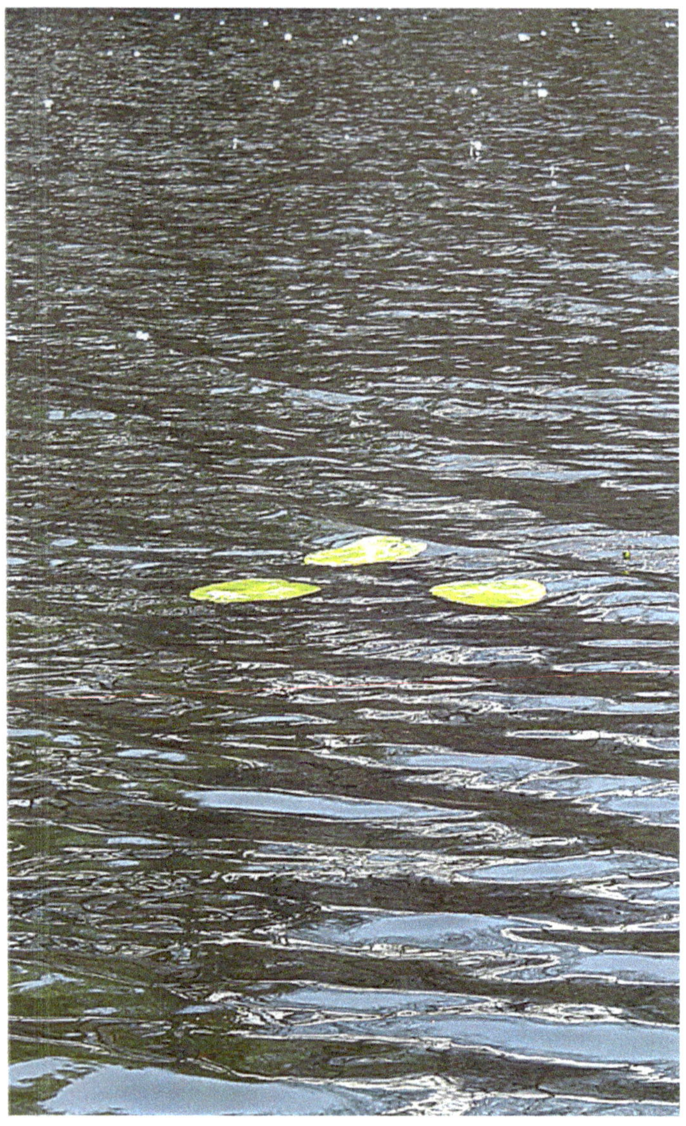

Non-Doing

"Non-doing has nothing to do with being indolent or
passive. Quite the contrary. It takes great courage and
energy to cultivate non-doing, both in stillness and in
activity. Nor is it easy to make a special time for non-doing
and to keep at it in the face of everything in our lives which
needs to be done."

— Jon Kabat-Zinn, *Wherever You Go, There You Are:
Mindfulness Meditation in Everyday Life*[45]

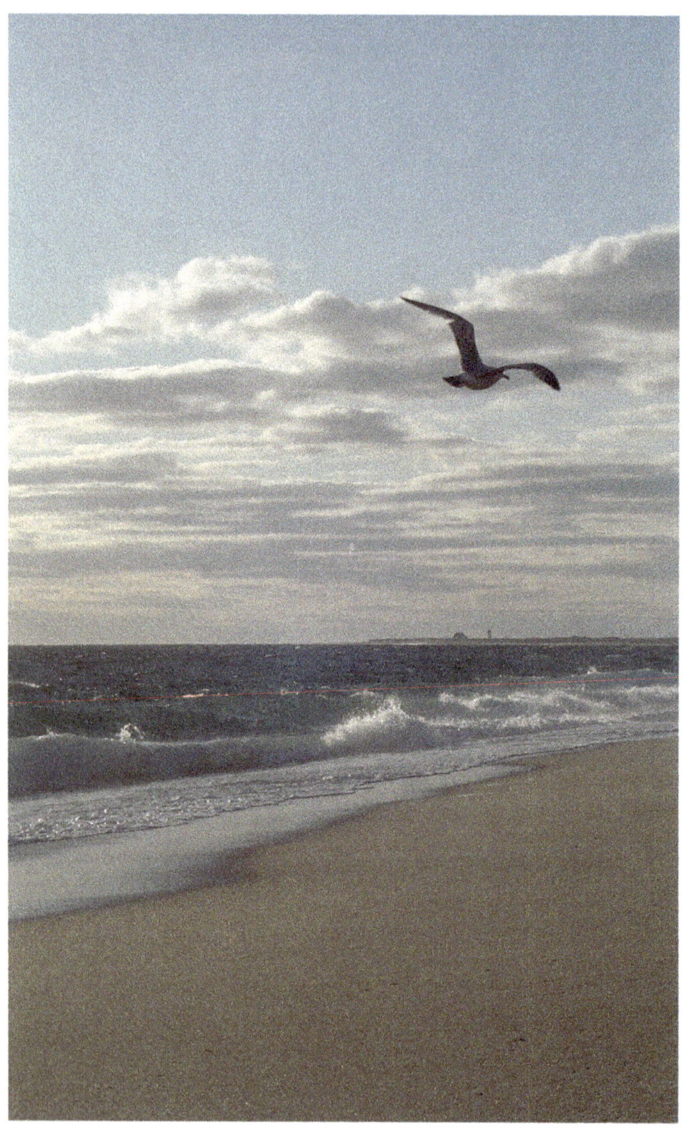

Touch the Earth

"Touch the earth, love the earth, her plains, her valleys, her hills, and her seas; rest your spirit in her solitary places. For the gifts of life are the earth's and they are given to all, and they are the songs of birds at daybreak, Orion and the Bear, and the dawn seen over the ocean from the beach."

— Henry Beston, *The Outermost House*[46]

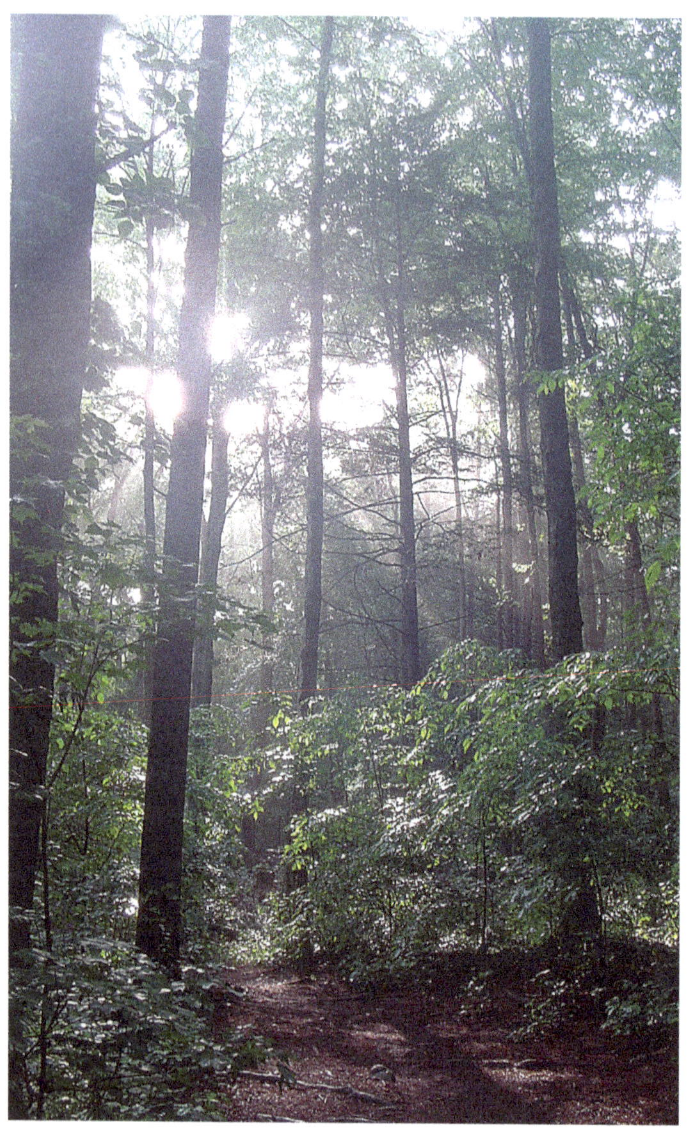

:: MAY

A Morning Walk

it is just past seven when I walk into the woods

a new day casts its light softly through treetops
and into still-dark places

the nighttime labors of small creatures wait like ghosts
in morning mist

the sun points the way, while bullfrogs and blue jays
serenade

the air is heavy and humid, but cool from last night's rain

forgotten raindrops fall from leaves and dance
across a stream

the forest smells familiar, its dampness and earth
like memories I can touch

they stay with me as I leave, the day so far ahead
from where I started

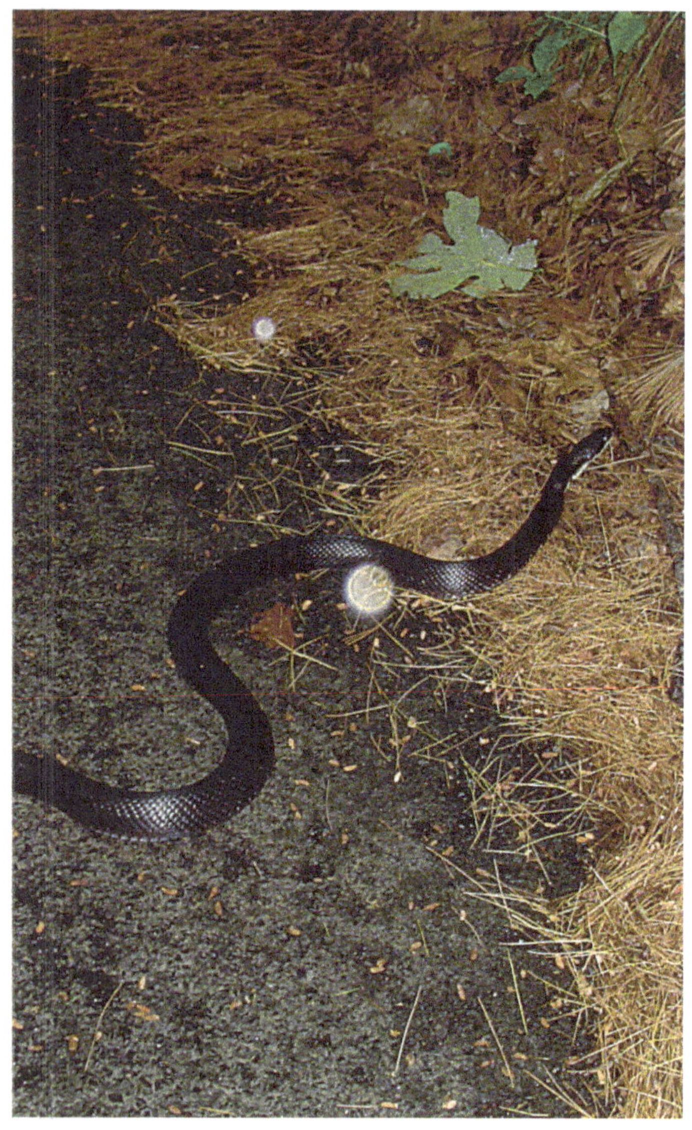

Thought Charmer

There are some meditations that cooperate, and some that just won't. There are some days I set foot into the woods and my thoughts slough away effortlessly. And there are days when the thoughts wrap around me like a boa, constricting my breath and my pace.

On days like that, when the thoughts insist on slithering about, I try to quiet them, coax them into submission—or scold them away like children. *Shhh!*

Yesterday was one of those days—perhaps the pinpoint focus of my workday had kept the thoughts too caged up.

"Was that a woodpecker?" the thoughts wondered.

EASTERN RAT SNAKE

Shhh.

"Chipmunk!"

Shhh.

"Butterfly. Butterfly. Butterfly."

Shhh. Shhh. Shhh.

"Is it warm enough for snakes yet?"

Shhh.

"Is it too cold for snakes?"

Shhh.

"Is that a snake?"

Shhh.

"Snake!"

Snake?

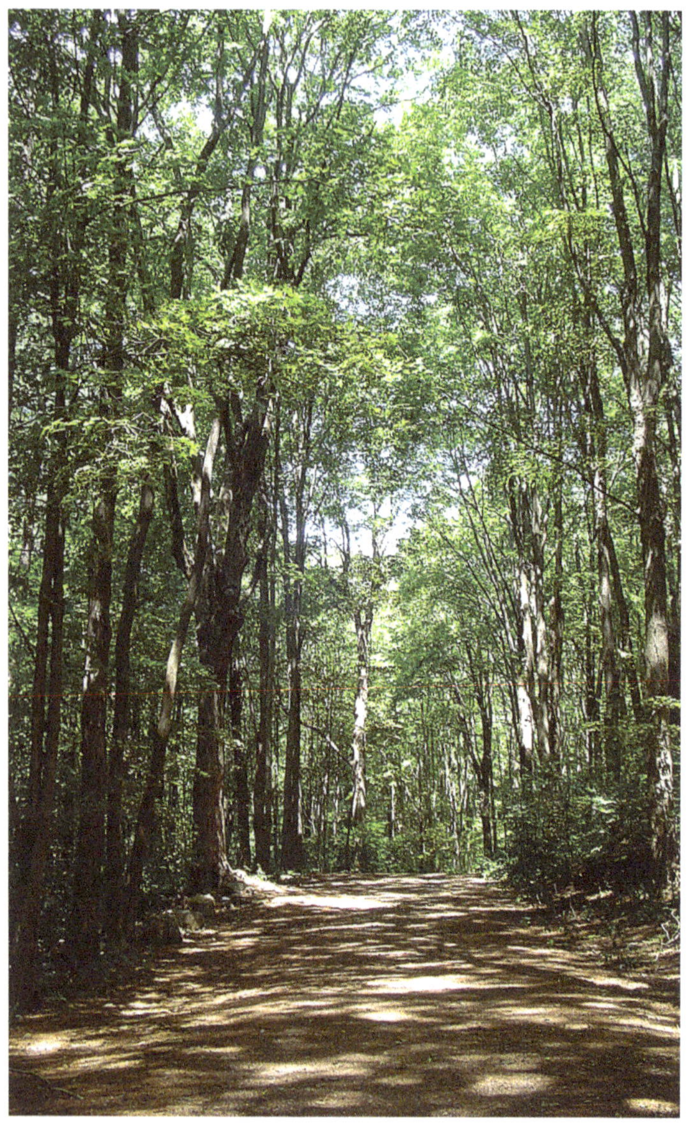

:: JUNE

Walk This Way

"I wished to walk this summer, but no one would walk with me. It is the perfect way of moving if you want to see into the life of things. It is the one way of freedom. If you go to a place on anything but your own feet you are taken there too fast, and miss a thousand delicate joys that were waiting for you by the wayside."

— Elizabeth Von Arnim, *The Adventures of Elizabeth in Rügen*[47]

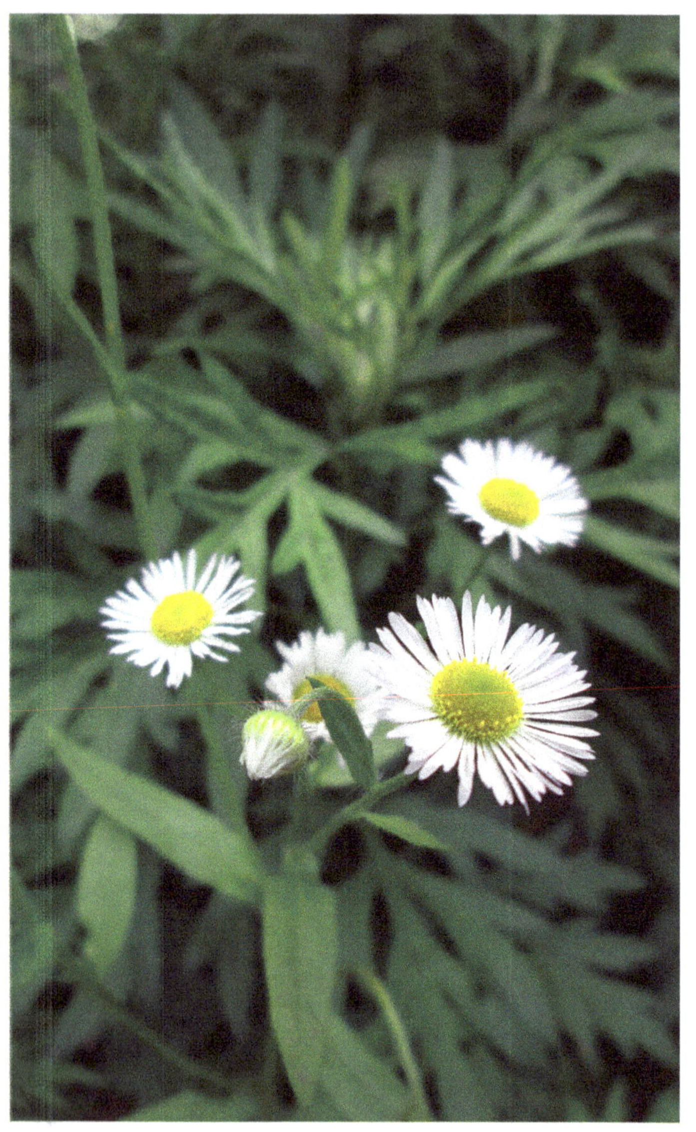

Summer Whisper

Yesterday, while I stood
knee-deep in meadow grass
to capture wild fleabane
and raspberries in bloom,
while a joyful bee dipped
and danced in front of me,
I almost missed the visitor
who came quickly down the path.
I think she thought I was
a flower—leftover perfumes from the day—
but stopped just shy of perceived pistil
when she realized I was not.
It took a while to focus.
I felt her before I saw,
so close was she
I felt the breeze
of her magic little wings.
"Summer's coming,"
the hummingbird whispered,
then floated off to
honeysuckle waiting
just nearby.

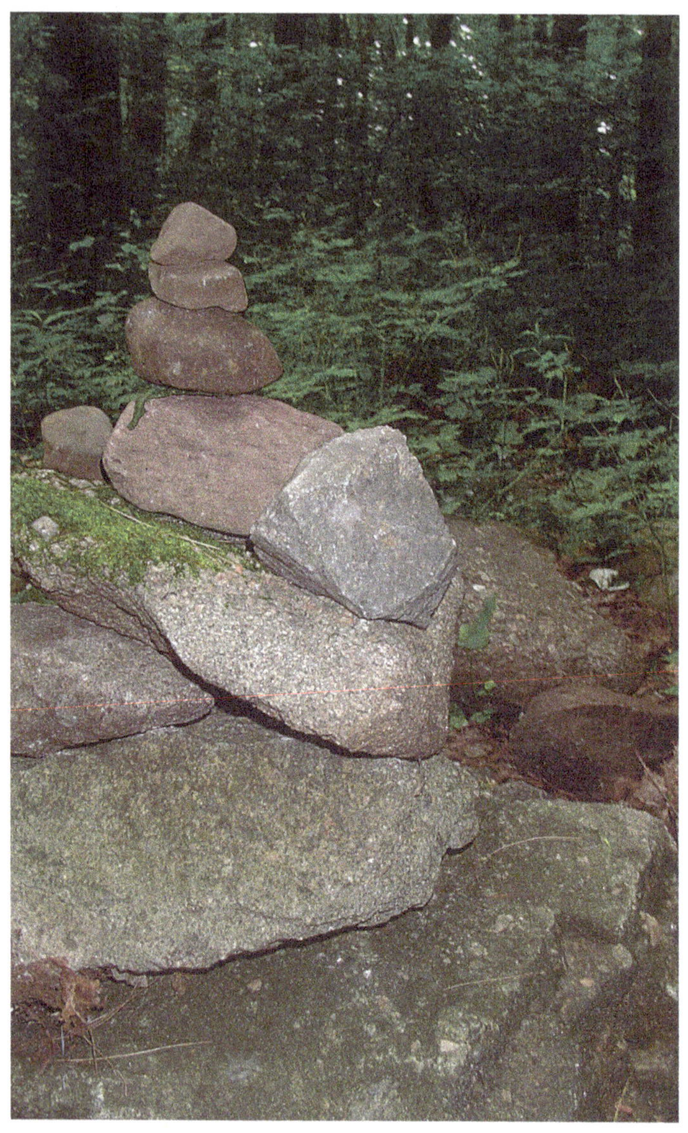

Nature's Way

In the woods where I walk, cairns appear. Sometimes weeks go between sightings, sometimes just days. Fellow walkers, in some whimsical collaboration with Nature, create these ancient monuments to time, ceremony, firmament, orientation.

Here, the cairns say, for whatever reason.

Here I am.

Here and now.

Look here. Go here.

For centuries, cairns both small and large, were used as grave markings, as defensive structures, and in religious ceremonies. In moderns times, they are known primarily as notes of direction—which way to go, where to turn, how to get from here to there.

When I walk in the woods, I walk in a circle. Left or right, this way or that, brings me back upon myself each time. And yet, these cairns still mark a way for me. From here, with cluttered thoughts and weary spirit, to there, with clear mind and lightened heart.

I never leave the woods without a new idea or a new perspective. And the cairns guide me. Here, they say, just come here.

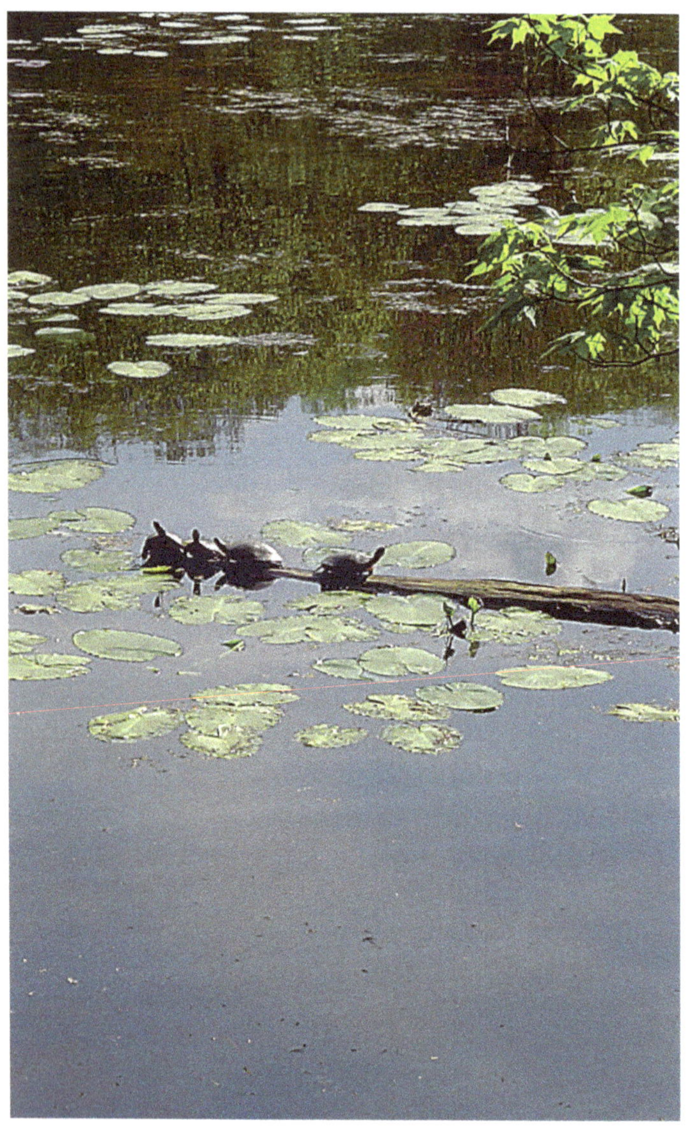

:: JULY

Permission Granted

I don't know what it is," I emailed my sister the other day. "I'm just in slow motion this week. My brain is excited with new ideas and expecting high productivity, but I'm just not feeling it."

"Slow and steady is sometimes better than fast paced," she emailed back. "Be the turtle this week!"

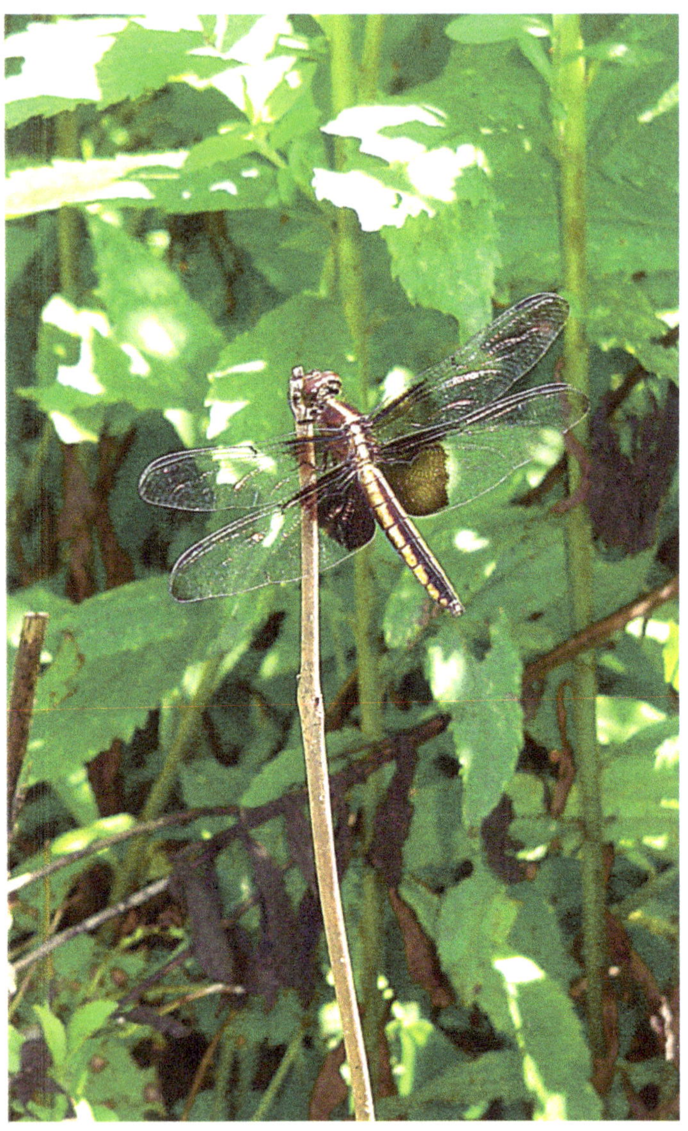

Answers: Here

There are moments in this life when I cannot find explanation. When searching for why becomes too much to bear. And so I walk off into the woods where, instead of answers, I just find peace.

If a dragonfly has shown up in your life, you may need some fresh air in regard to something emotional. You may need to gain a new perspective or make a change…. Are you resisting change when you shouldn't? Dragonflies remind us that we are light and can reflect the light in powerful ways if we chose to do so. "Let there be light" is the divine prompting to use the creative imagination as a force within your life.

Life is never quite the way it appears, but it is always filled with light and color. Dragonfly can help you see through your illusions and thus allow your own light to shine forth. Dragonfly brings the brightness of transformation and the wonder of colorful new vision.

— Ted Andrews, *Animal Speak: The Spiritual & Magical Powers of Creatures Great and Small*[48]

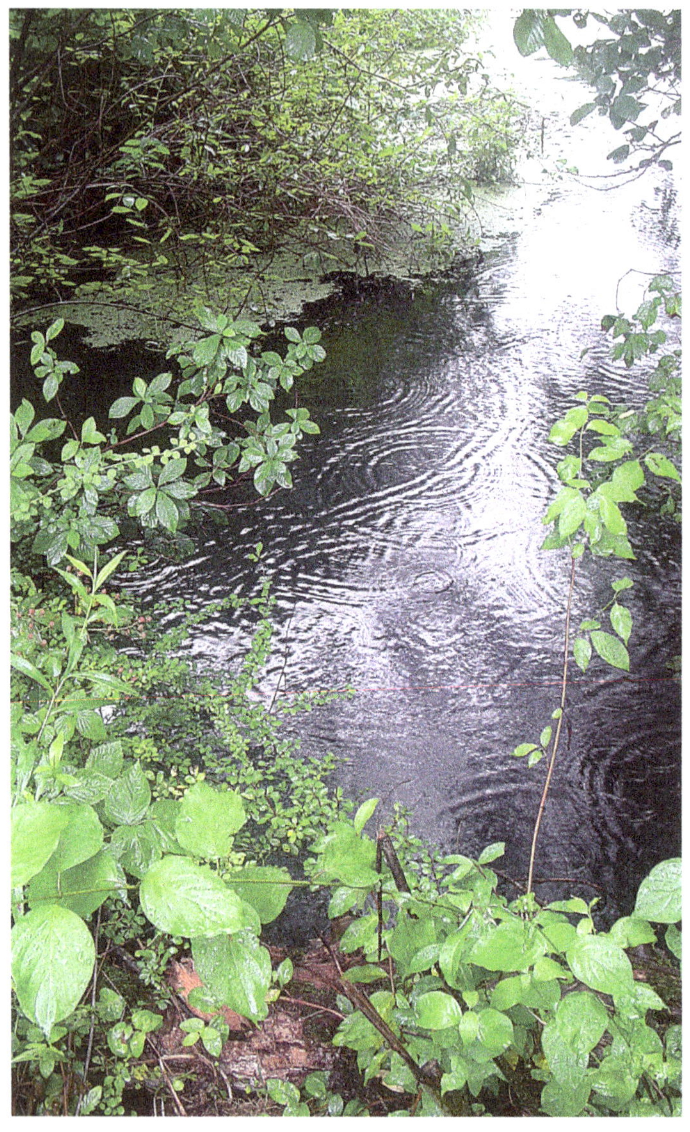

Connections

"Our ancient experience confirms it at every instant: everything is linked together, everything is inseparable."

— Dalai Lama, *The Path to Tranquility*[49]

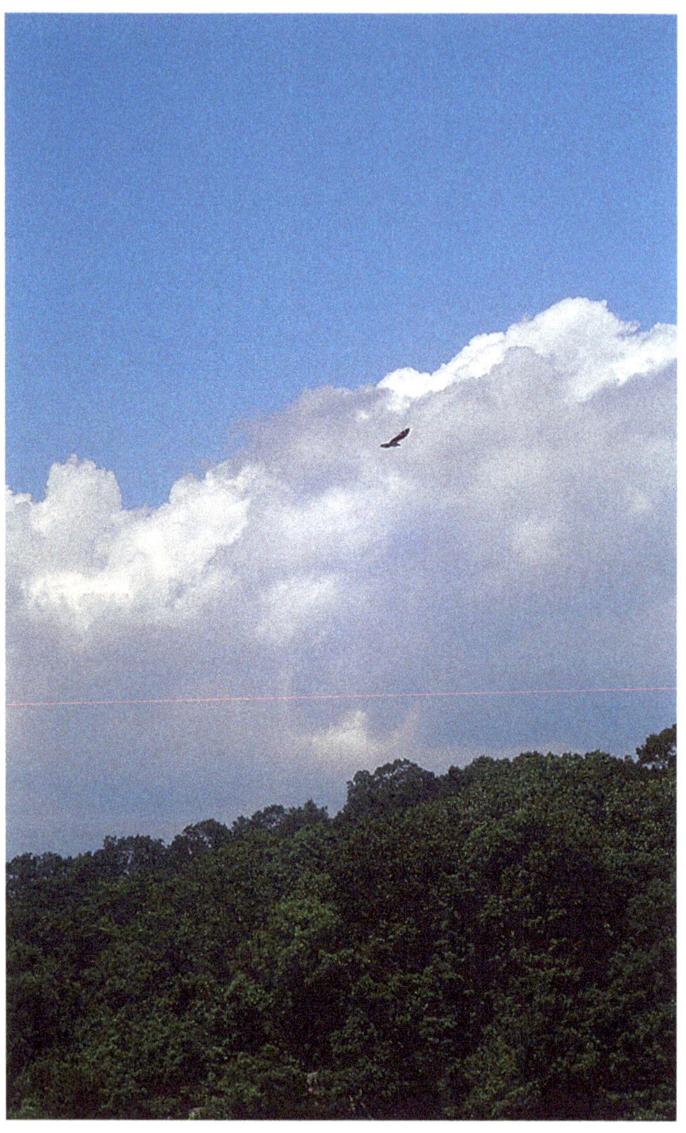

No Other Choice

When the Universe serves up a breezy, 70-degree morning in the middle of the summer, you have no other choice but to get outside and wrap yourself up in it for a while.

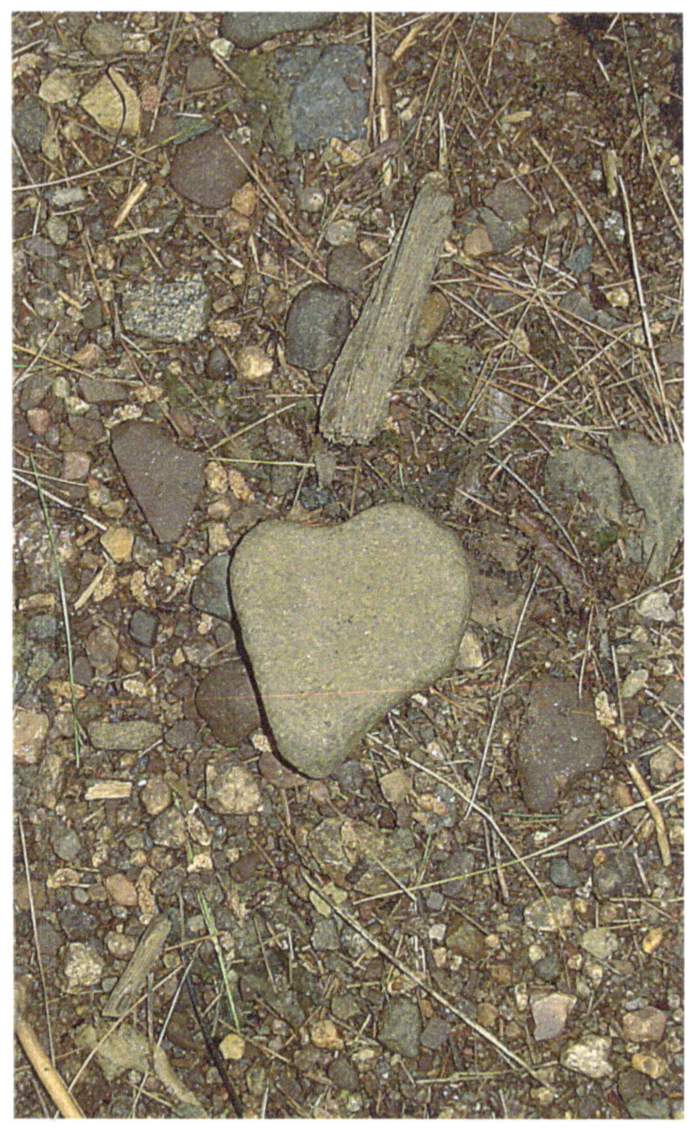

Divine Assistance

I was walking with a burden this week. No bigger or smaller than anyone else's, it was just a burden. The kind that takes up residence sometimes and refuses to leave.

So on Sunday, I asked the Universe for help—"Help me find peace with this," I said out loud as I made my way along the path. But the burden voiced its opinions loudly for most of the hour...with much repetition. Near the end of my walk, a sturdy breeze wound its way through the trees, up the path, into my face and through my hair. "Cool your temper," it whispered. "Shhhhhhh."

On Monday, the burden returned, early in the morning and sat with me all day. I went to the woods and asked the Universe again—"Help me find peace with this," wondering if She would listen to my request this time. Near the footbridge, a butterfly floated back and forth, and I asked her to come closer. She flitted here and there for a while, then sat gently down right in front of me for several shutter snaps. "It will come to you," the Universe whispered. "Have patience."

On Tuesday, the burden returned once more. "What about this? What about that? Remember this? Remember that?" it demanded, getting heavier and heavier as I walked. "Help me find peace with this," I asked again, looking up to the sky for some kind of guidance. Above me, eight ospreys danced and sang—making great joyful loops in the sky. "Let it go," the Universe whispered. "Find joy."

On Wednesday, the burden returned again. But it was quieter now. Not as intrusive, but still around enough to notice. "I have to find peace with this," I said out loud as I watched my steps along the path. There, in front of me, was a heart-shaped rock—set out as if to catch my eye. "Some things are more important," the Universe whispered. "Love."

I tucked it in my pocket and have felt lighter ever since.

Solution

A cross almost 2500 years of time, the Greek philosopher Diogenes of Sinope whispers *solvitur ambulando*—it is solved by walking—and so it is.

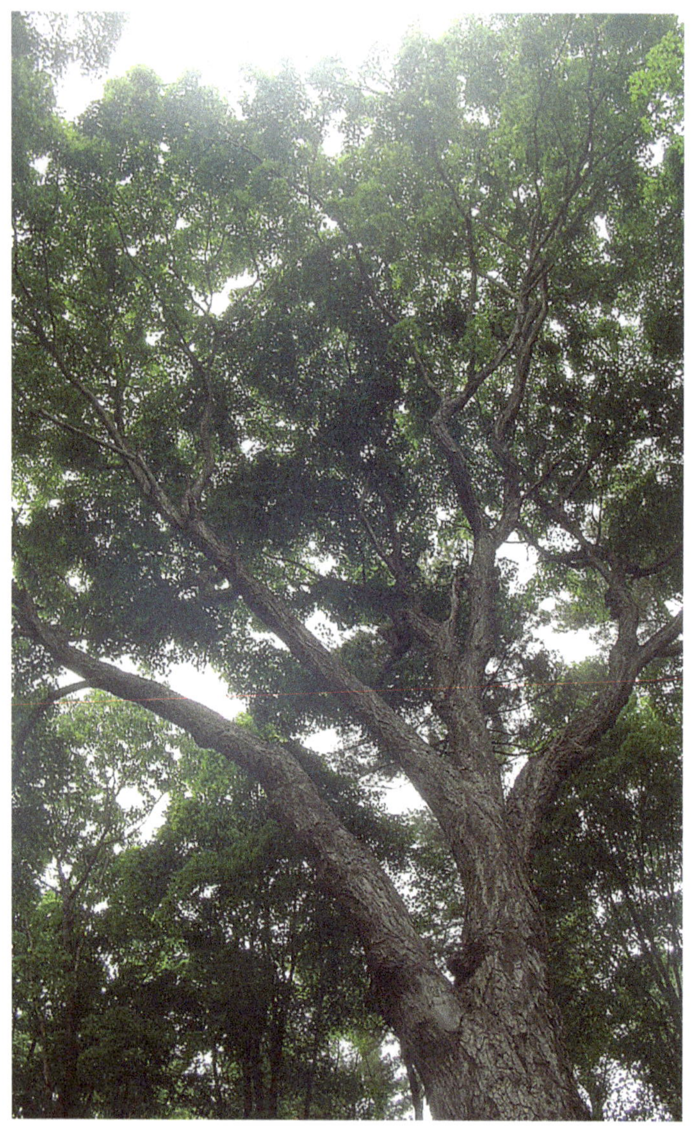

:: AUGUST

Seize Earth by the Pole

In my favorite Robert Frost poem, "On a Tree Fallen Across the Road," we learn of a tree felled by sudden winter winds. Its impeding presence on the snow-full path becomes analogy for life's challenges and our responses.

How many times have you come upon a similar obstacle that seems determined to stop you from moving forward?

Such was the case for me a few weeks ago. A tree fell in the middle of my path and asked, "who do you think you are?"

At first, I resisted.

This is a good and familiar path. I want to stay here.

Surely I can move this tree and continue on my way.

But there was a louder voice that let me know I needed heed this call for change. It was time to be on a different path, whether I liked it, or not. Whether I was ready for it, or not.

Rather than sit with the familiar hesitation of these course corrections, I embraced it…thanked the path and honored the message of the tree.

And so it was this morning that I found myself on a different path, surrounded by a new community, and breathing joy.

My sister introduced me to Frost's poem "On a Tree Fallen Across the Road," hand-written on the inside of a twenty-something birthday card. His beautiful interplay of Nature and life observations has stayed with me since, a constant reminder that the challenges we face at any age offer the blessing of new directions. If there were a poem to fold up and keep close to heart, this would be it.[50]

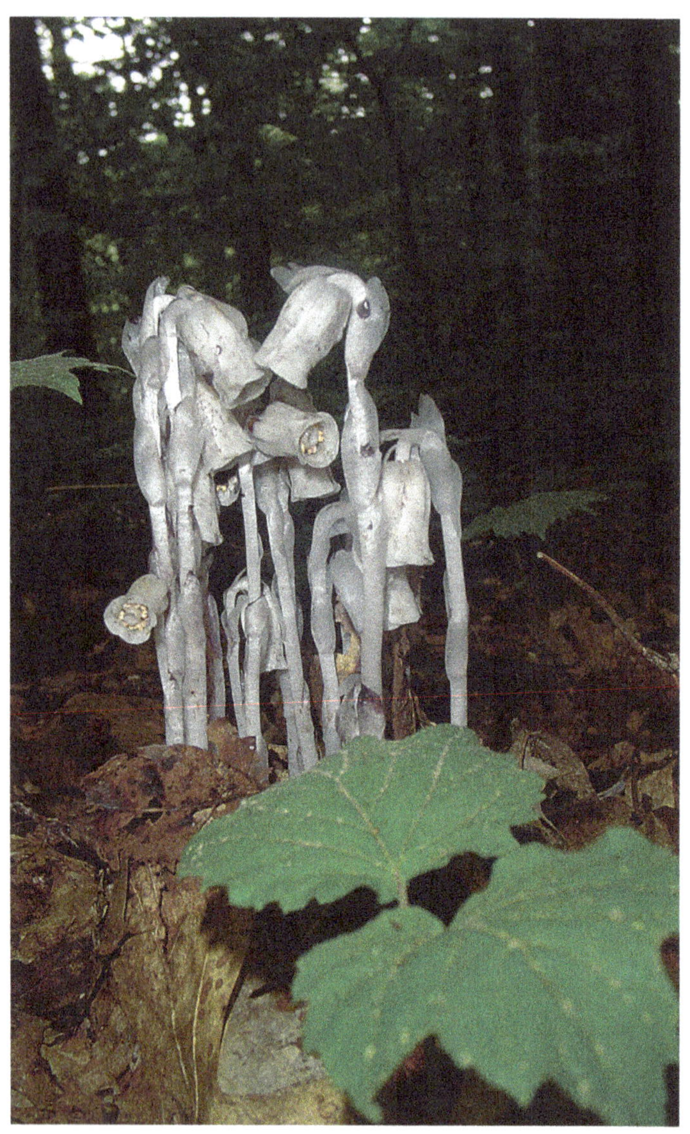

An Eastern Meditation?

This weekend, a stop at the local organic farm yielded some yummy late summer treats: cucumbers, Swiss chard, green beans, a miniature watermelon, and two small heads of cabbage.

It was a dry, 70-degree afternoon with just enough of a breeze to appease my summer-weary spirit, and I could not resist a chance to visit the woods for a walk afterwards.

It had been a while since I quieted my mind with a long walk, so I stepped onto the path with much anticipation.

It didn't take long to fall into a familiar rhythm—the neglected and random thoughts each forcing themselves to the front so quickly they became a dull hum by the time I reached the top of the first hill.

At that point, it's always easy for me to stop paying attention to them and instead begin careful attention to the moment right in front me of.

The blue jay.

The oak tree.

INDIAN PIPE (or GHOST PLANT)

The pine needles.

The goldenrod.

My attention. My mantra.

bird

branch

breeze

bee

bud

bug

buzz

"I should make kimchi!"

The thought stepped up so loudly, it was as if there was someone right next to me!
Meditation seems to be that way—it is, and then it isn't.

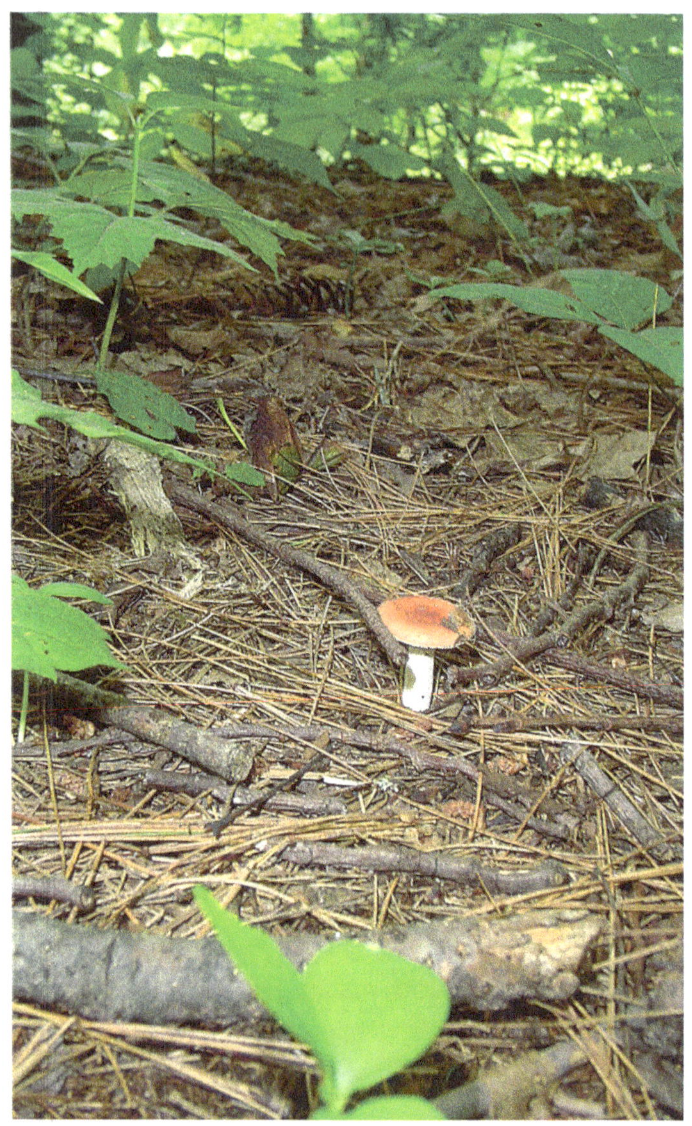

Seeing Things

L ong before I found the courage to wander in the woods alone, Lynda was walking in the woods. When we meet up, usually over piles of paper at the local print shop, she is always excited to show me her photos—the ones she takes on her long walks along hidden paths in local woods.

She climbs trees and crouches to the ground. She crawls into hollowed-out trunks and sits patiently with frogs and robin eggs. She spends hours visiting the forest, getting to know the leaf, the insect, the moss.

I was thinking about Lynda today, as I crouched under a branch to snap a photo of a mushroom. There was a cobweb wrapped around my wrist and rain dripping down my back, and I knew I would not be seeing the world that way if she hadn't traveled the path before me.

It is said we are made up of everything we have ever seen, thought, felt, spoken, or done, and on the subconscious level, all of this becomes a permanent part of us, engraved on our grey cells forever. If this experience takes place in Nature, we are much more than we were before, and the better for it.

— Cathy Johnson, *The Naturalist's Path*[51]

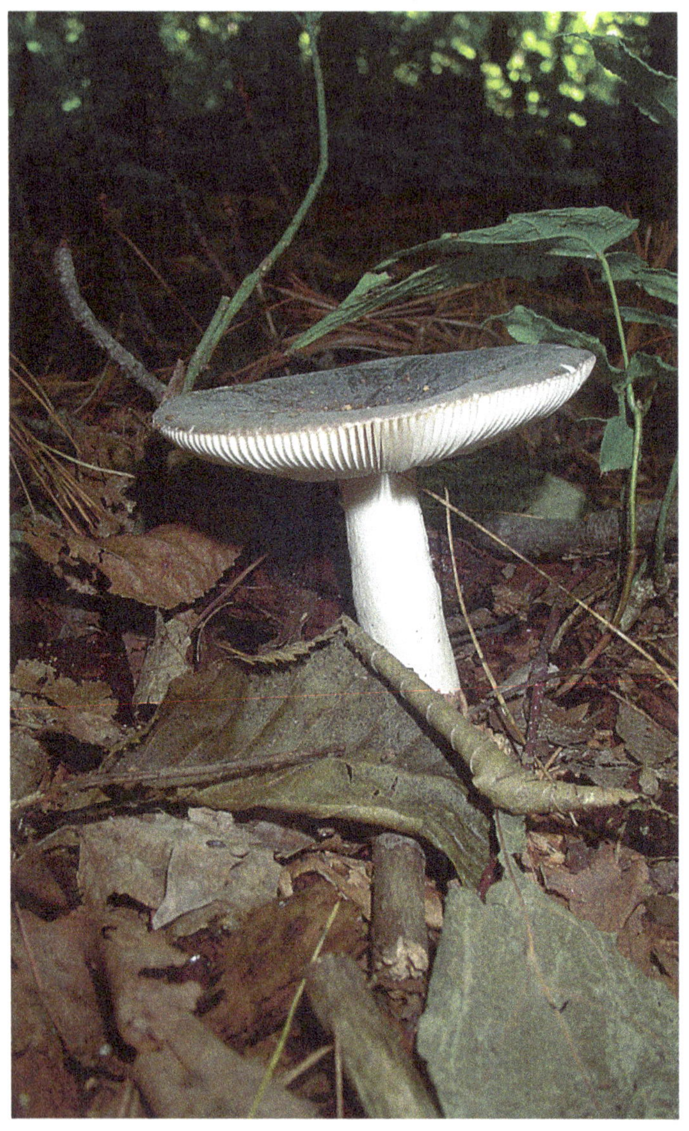

Ode to Fungi

On bended knee
I bow to your

creativity
fertility
singularity
your
simplicity
and dignity
...absurdity?

Divinity.

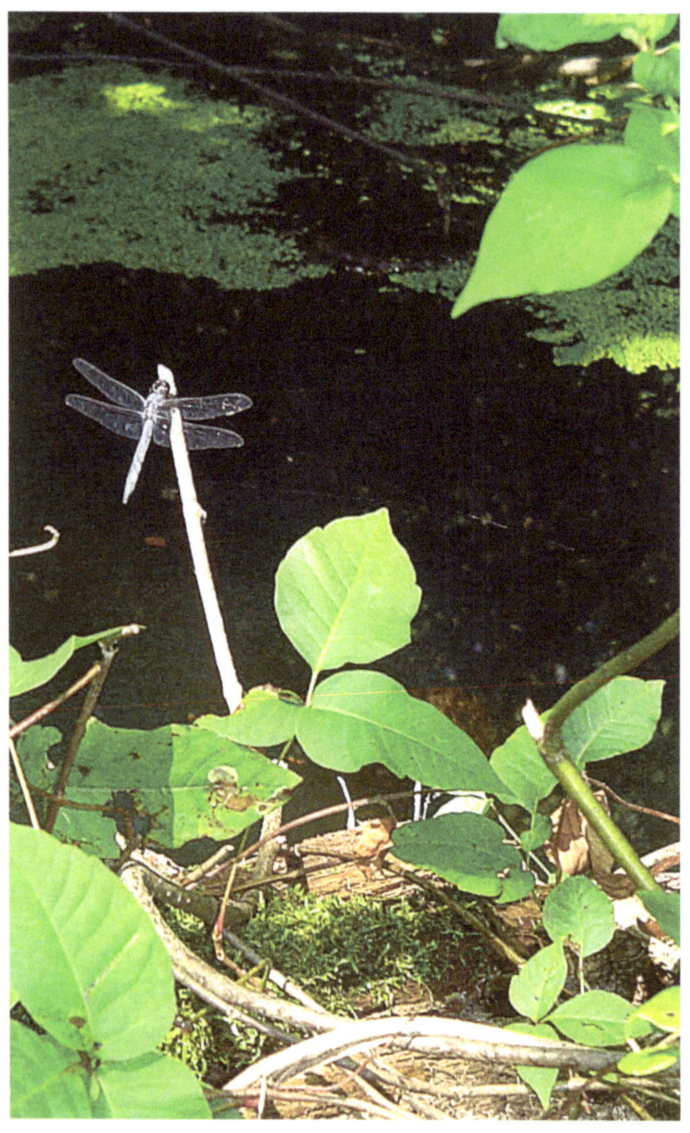

:: SEPTEMBER

In the Moment

"Why do we have to take care of the present moment?...It is where all the wonder is possible. You cannot go to the past and drink a cup of tea. You cannot go to the future to drink a cup of tea. But *now*, we are drinking a cup of tea."

— Brother Phap Huy[52]

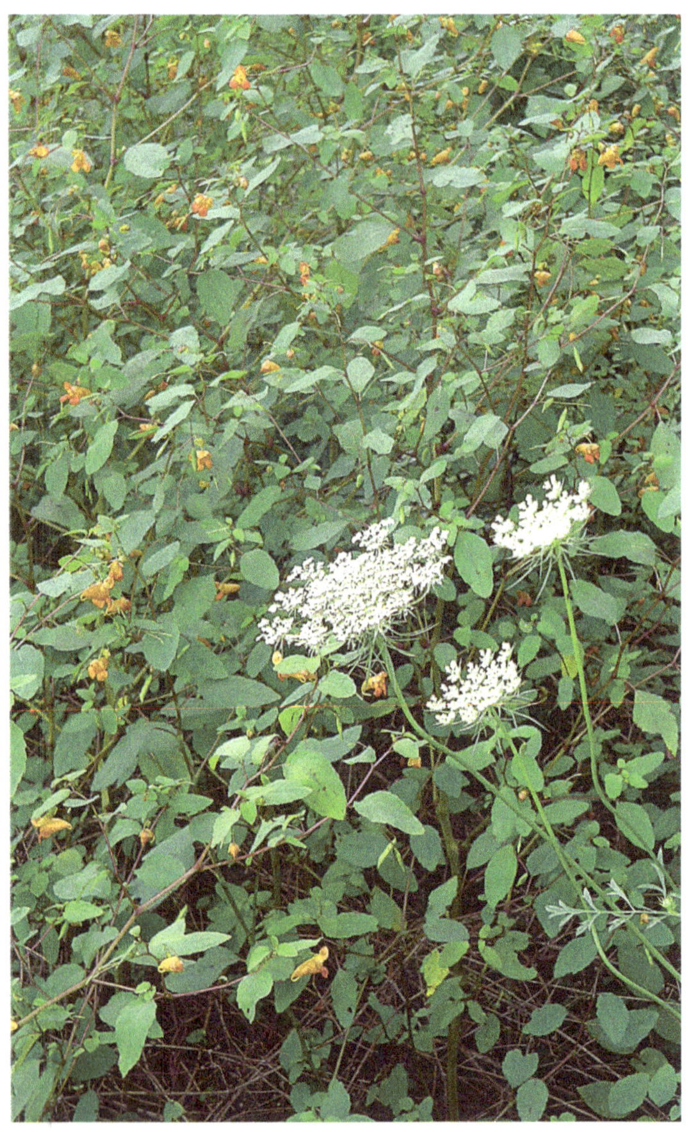

The Tail End of a Moment

I heard your footsteps as

I stopped to smell the roses…

Jewelweed.

Queen Anne's Lace.

Someone's coming!

Don't look up.

Be in the moment.

Right here.

Jewelweed.

Queen Anne's Lace.

I only caught a glimpse of your tail

as you slipped into the forest ahead.

Fox.

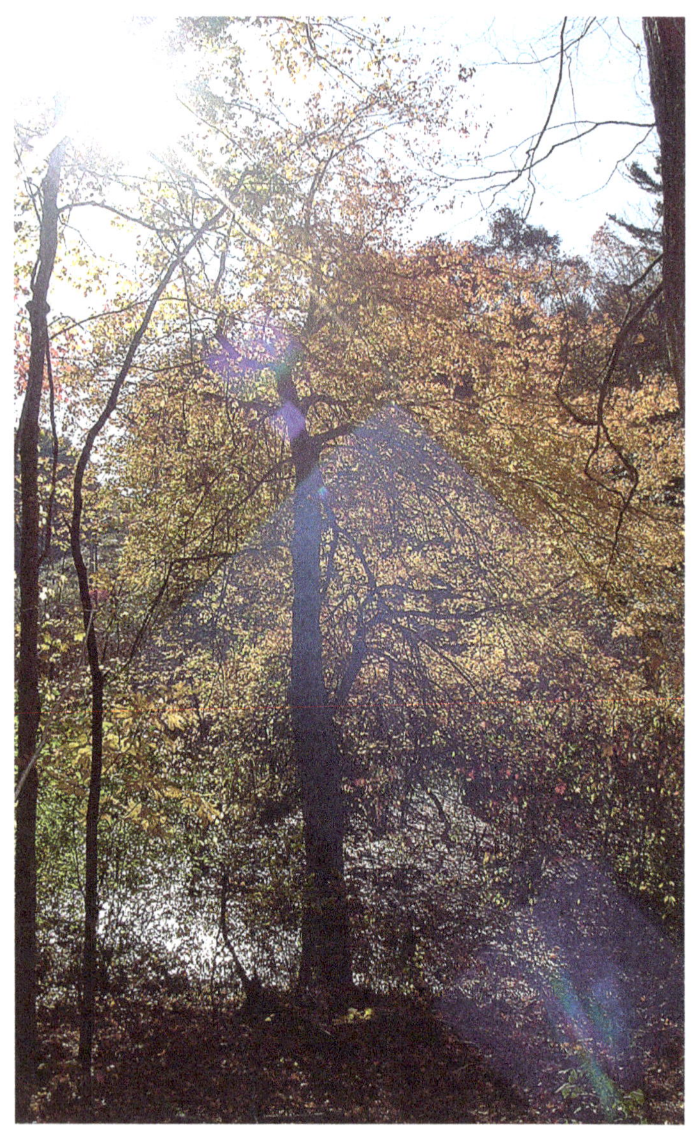

:: OCTOBER

Afire with God

"Earth's crammed with heaven,
And every common bush afire with God...."

— Elizabeth Barrett Browning[53]

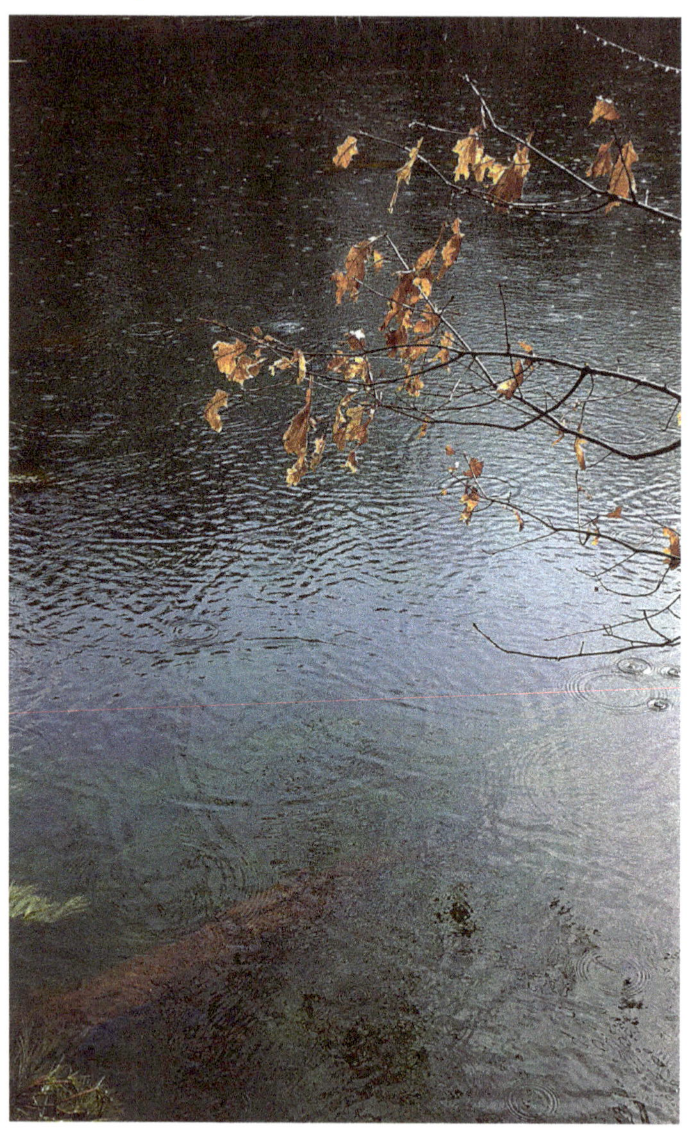

Walking with Rain

The clouds arrived yesterday afternoon and their timing was perfect. It had been a while since I'd been to the woods...even longer still since the rain was my companion.

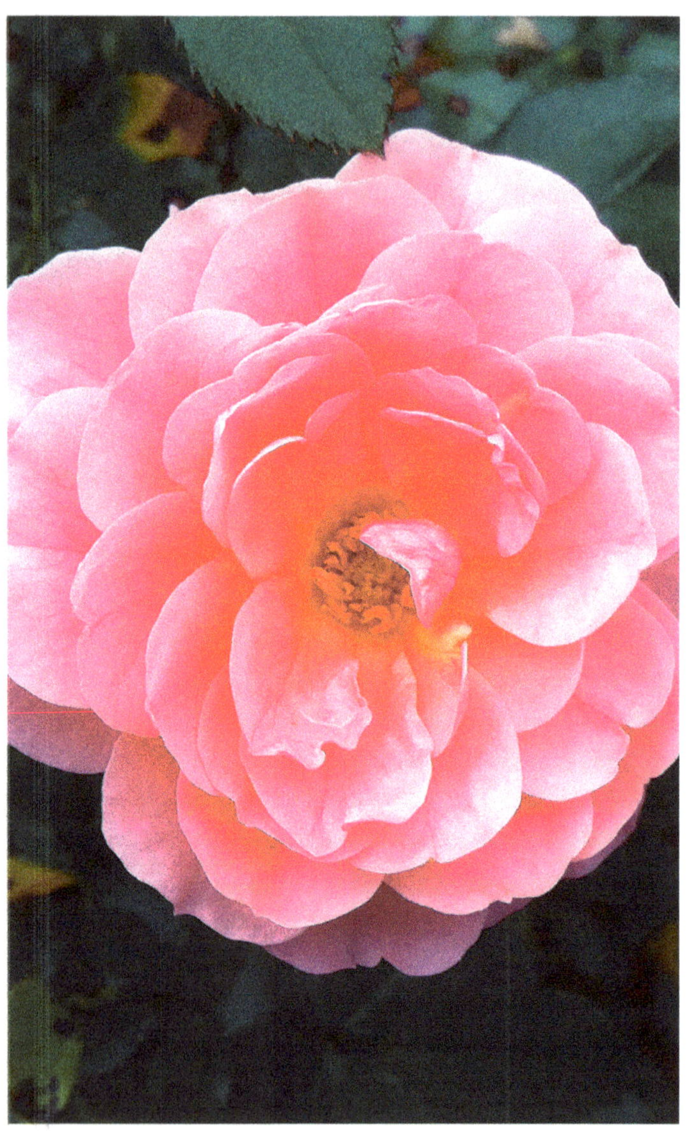

:: NOVEMBER

Note to Self: Smell Roses

I t was nearly eleven o'clock in the morning before I realized I had not spent one mindful moment since I'd pulled myself out of bed at four. From the second my feet touched the cold, wood floor, I'd been "on."

On autopilot, I suppose: brush teeth, pull on sweatshirt (and socks for cold feet), turn on computer, make coffee, feed the cat, work.

Work. Work. Work. Work. Work…eleven?

That's pretty much how the morning went.

My mind was so full of other things, I neglected the morning meditation that has been part of the routine since July.

I forgot the candle lighting, the prayer, the stillness, the incense, the affirmations. I erased "afternoon walk" from the To Do list for lack of time.

And I forgot that all of that makes all of the other stuff more balanced…and less likely to stick itself in the knot that tangles in my shoulders.

A friend commented yesterday that we need to at least LOOK at the roses as we pass by them.

But smelling…so much better…is breathing, and back to where I should have been at four.

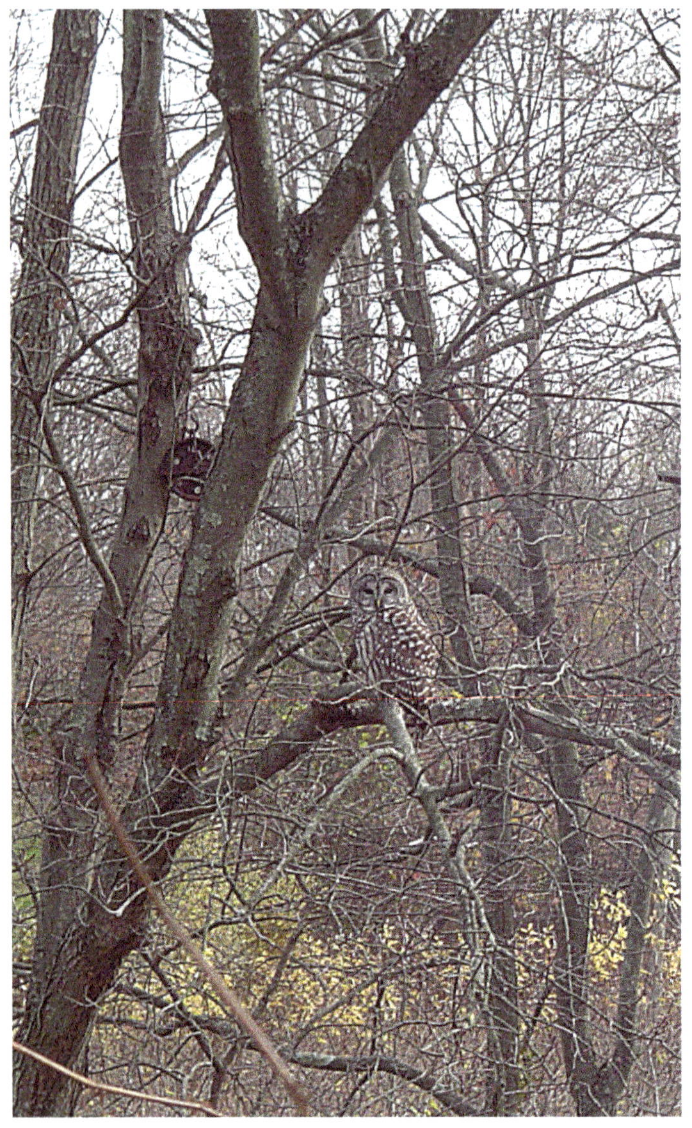

Guardians

Like my breath in yoga, I am both expanding
and contracting today.

Full inhales of breath open me up and stretch me farther.

Deep exhales draw me inside, grounded.

A desire to set my writing out into the world has me
reaching, taking bolder steps. Stating my intentions clearly
and with full purpose like full breath.

At the same time, recent health concerns find me going
inward, centering myself and my thoughts on healing.
Quietly meditating on positive and easy outcomes.

This morning,

as I inhale

and exhale

I spy a barred owl perched upon a branch outside my
window. It is the second day she has kept watch, and it is
magical.

*"The owl is the bird of magic and darkness, of prophecy
and wisdom," writes Ted Andrews in Animal Speak: The
Spiritual & Magical Powers of Creatures Great and Small.
"Over time, the owl has been associated with the feminine,
the moon, the night, fertility, higher wisdom, protection,
clairvoyance. It is believed to have healing powers, and
is able to extract secrets from the darkness of the human
spirit. Owl brings with it the message of truth and
awareness."*[54]

In my breath today there is both. There is an inhale of
truth as I claim my words and my story as my own to tell.
There is an exhale of awareness as I listen quietly to what
my body needs to say, to the story it has to tell. And so this
morning,

as I inhale

and exhale

It is no surprise that my spirit guide, the hawk, alights on
a tree just three branches above the owl. Hawk is always with
me, guiding, protecting. Hawk "can wake visionary power
and lead you to your life purpose," Andrews explains. "It is
the messenger bird. Whenever it shows up, pay attention.
There is a message coming."[55]

A message. A blessing. And breath.

Namaste.

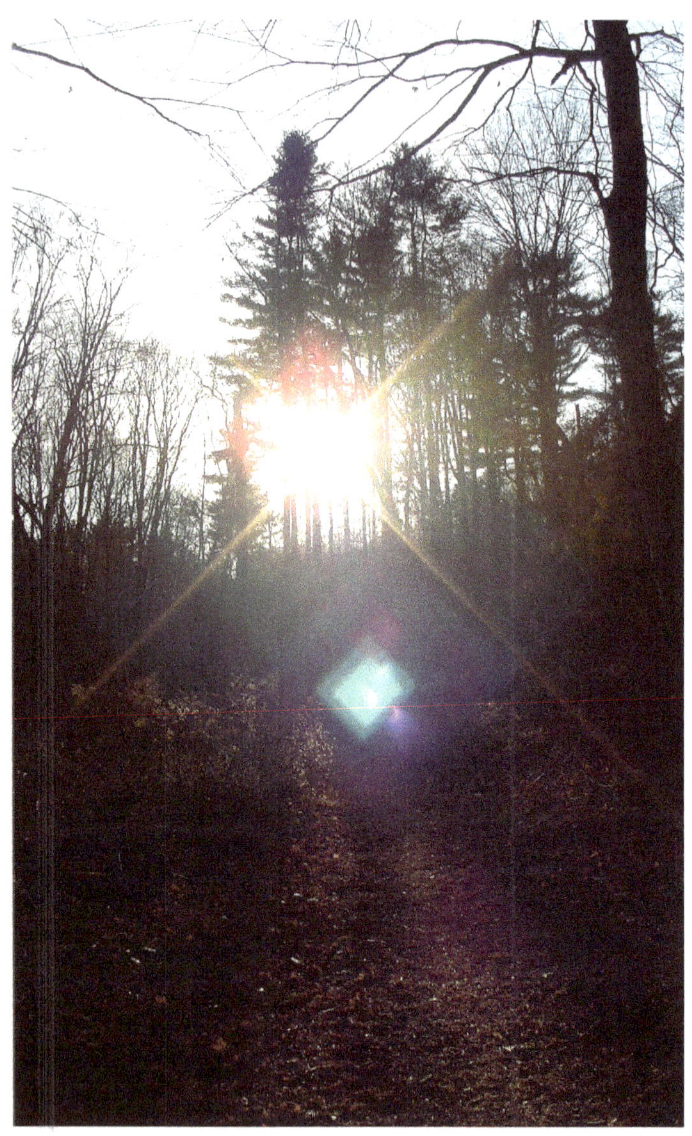

:: DECEMBER

What Lies before Us

I was walking in the woods this afternoon. It was about three o'clock or so, and I was heading due west—I know this because the sun was perfectly and directly staring me in the face such that I could not see in front of me. There was a path at my feet, that much I knew, but there was not much beyond the trail except darkness and shadow. Yet I kept walking, each step as sure as the last that there would be path to meet me as I made my way forward.

It reminded me of the conversation I had with my dentist's receptionist yesterday. I was scheduling a cleaning for next year, *next* November.

"Are you available on the 19th?" she asked. "2:30?"

"Yes," I said, pretty sure I didn't have any plans.

As she wrote my name and phone number down on next year's calendar, I thought: that's one confident assumption, isn't it?

I will be here. I will be HERE in a year.

2:30 p.m. will still be a negotiable time in my daily schedule.

I will have the same phone number and live in the same town, now the place I have called "home" for 21 years.

I take them for granted, I think. These confidences. Who and where and what I will be a year from now. Don't we all?

A little father down the path, I met an older man named Jim. While his dog Yardley and I played fetch, Jim told me about his wife who had lost her eyesight and now relies on Yardley for assistance. She recently spoke to a class of college students, he told me, about what it was like to lose her eyesight so late in life.

She cannot see in front of her, and yet she moves forward—making her way in the world with aplomb and the love of good companions.

Perhaps that's all it takes to keep moving forward. To keep walking on this path whether we can see what's ahead or not: a little self-assurance and lots of love.

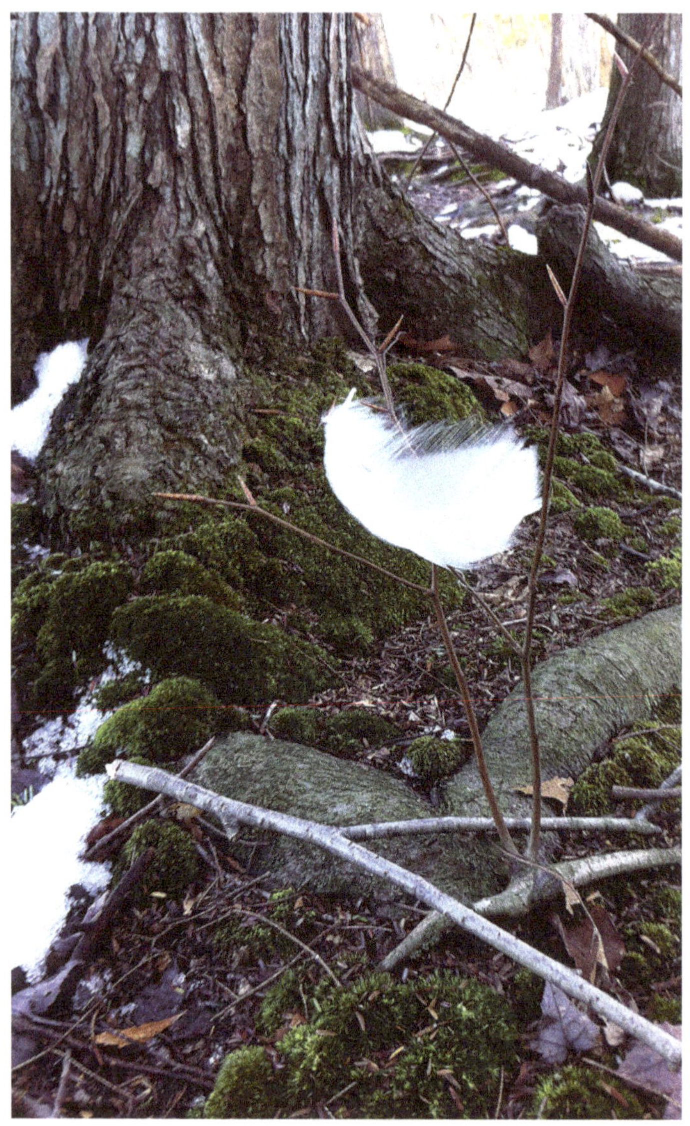

Evidence of Fairies

There is a path I walk along
that seems of ancient time.
Low-bent branches
and carpets of moss.
A convocation of
creatures and spirits
who move about
with rustles of leaves.
Makeshift footbridges
cross giggling streams
and a walking stick
props itself against
a century-old tree as if
a visitor sits there I cannot see.
And every now and then,
I am certain I find
evidence of fairies.

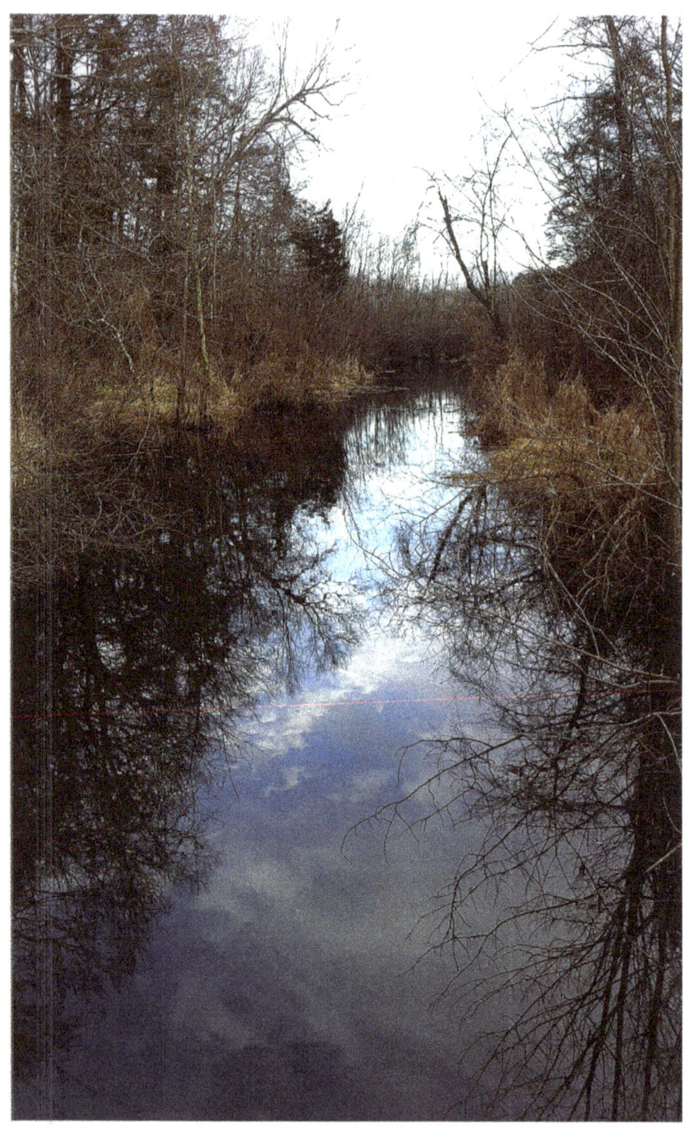

:: JANUARY

Through the Looking Glass

"Love the moment and the energy of that moment
will spread beyond all boundaries."[56]

— Corita Kent

LOVE THE MOMENT, CORITA, SERIGRAPH, 1977. REPRODUCTION
PERMISSION OF THE CORITA ART CENTER, IMMACULATE HEART
COMMUNITY, LOS ANGELES.

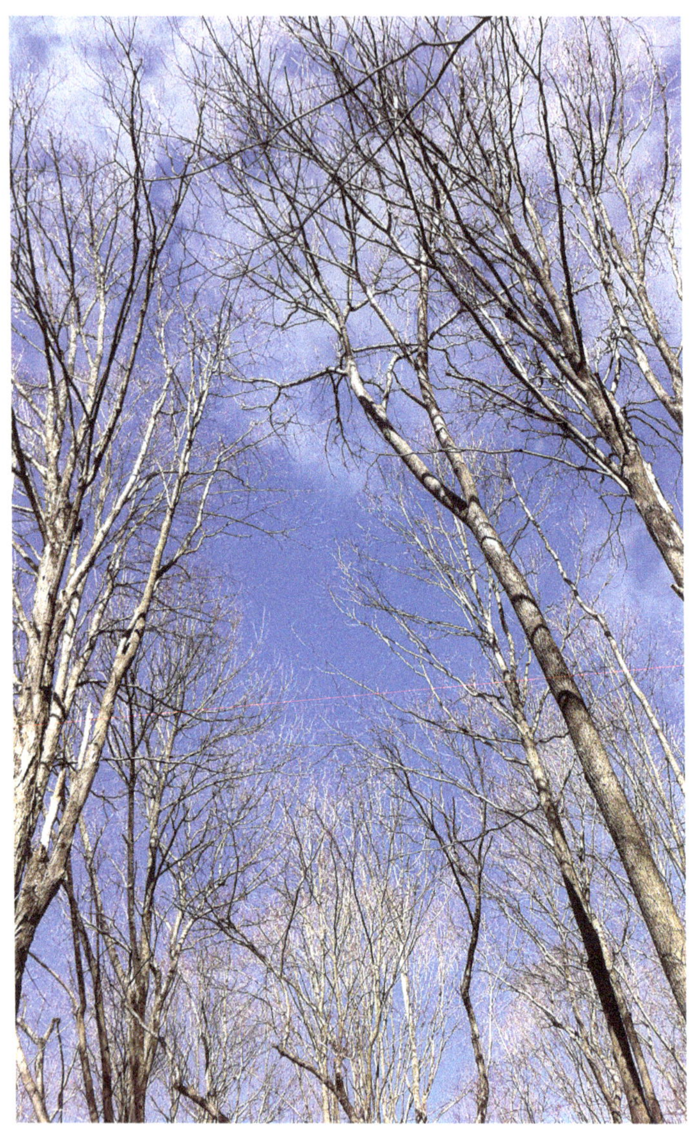

Look Up

I was so deeply into you

I almost missed the sky.

Until a whisper called my name

and heaven caught my eye.

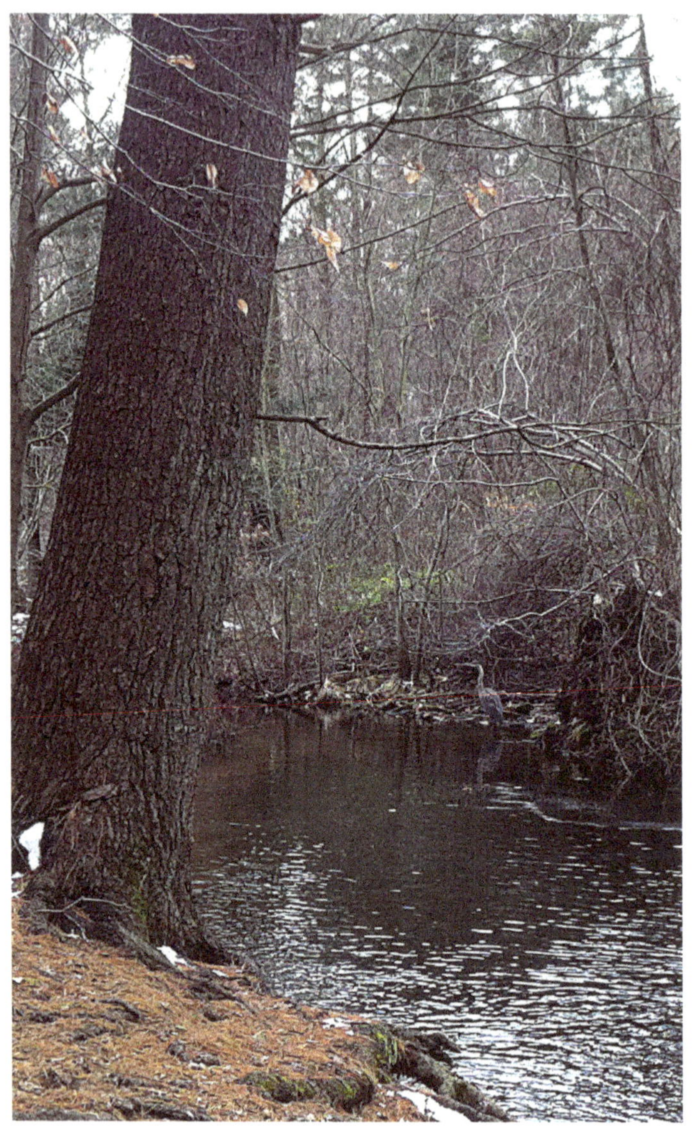

A Chance Sighting

I was feeling rather aimless yesterday—from the start of the day at work to the meandering afternoon of house chores. At two o'clock, I set off into the woods for a walk, thinking that might calm my restless spirit, but it remained just so.

Instead of going right, I went left. Instead of the familiar path, I followed a little foot track that curved this way and that in the snow. I doubled back to where I started, once, twice, then found my way to the path by the stream and thirsty trees.

Overhead a heron, in graceful and primordial ease, set down onto a branch of a pine felled in the fall storms. I stopped. Quiet. Watching as she slowly and meditatively scanned the water passing in front of her.

She saw me then and softly walked several feet down the stream, and I followed. We danced this way, in quiet ballet, until a bend in the river I could not pass.

She continued on her way and I on mine—the chance encounter a salve to my rambling mind, now suddenly quiet.

They are symbols of balance and they represent an ability to progress and evolve....The long thin legs of the heron reflect that you don't need great massive pillars to remain stable, but you must be able to stand on your own.

When it feeds, it stands in the water, reflecting a connection to the earth—while implying the exploration of other dimensions on the earth (water element). It is important for anyone with a heron totem to explore various activities and dimensions of earth life. On the surface, this may seem a form of dabbling, but those with heron totems are wonderfully successful at being the traditional "jack of all trades."

This ability enables them to follow their own path. Most people will never be able to live the way heron people do. It is not a structured way, and does not seem to have stability and security to it. It is, though, just a matter of perspective. There is security in heron medicine, for it gives the ability to do a variety of tasks. If one way does not work, then another will.

— Ted Andrews, *Animal Speak: The Spiritual & Magical Powers of Creatures Great and Small*[57]

And There Truth

"There is no path to truth, it must come to you. Truth can come to you only when your mind and heart are simple, clear, and there is love in your heart; not if your heart is filled with the things of the mind."

— Jiddu Krishnamurti, *The Book of Life: Daily Meditations with Krishnamurti*[58]

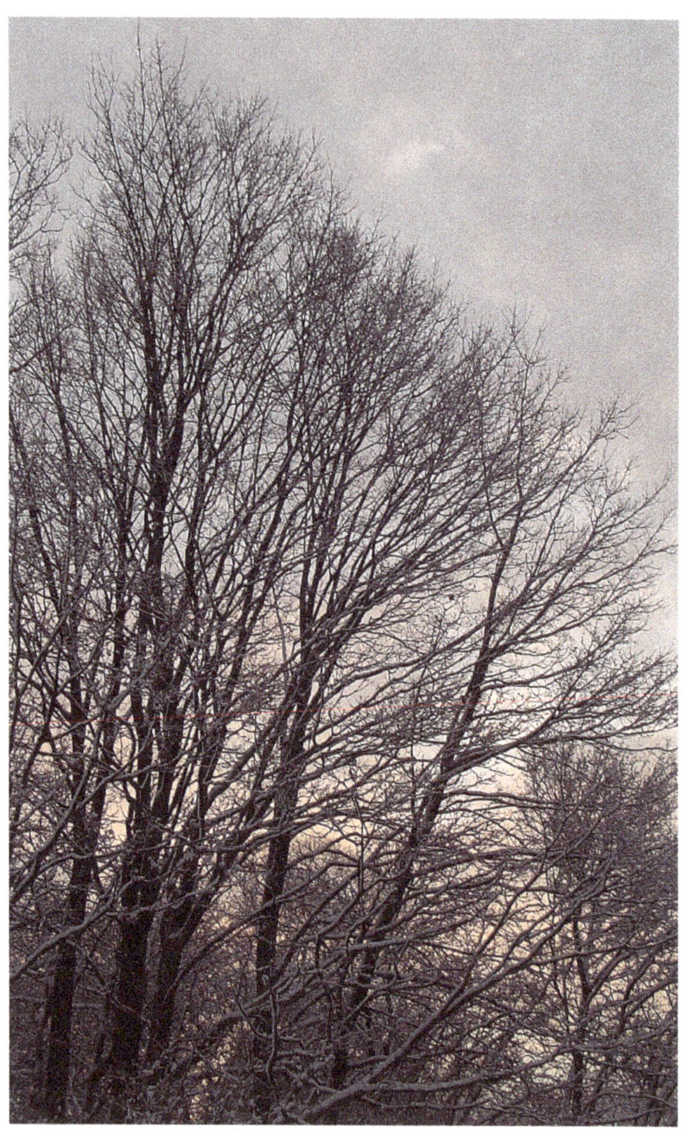

:: FEBRUARY

Lessons in Snow

There was no chance to go to the woods yesterday. By midday, the impending blizzard had been teasing us with feather-soft snow for hours, luring us into a false but hopeful sense that this is all it had to offer. But the weather reports were grim; even the independent, non-apocalyptic forecasts were ominous.

I was as prepared as I could be: the battery-operated lamp, the pile of books, the familiar assortment of provisions, the bottle of wine.

Part of the preparation was shoveling. I figured if I did a frequent pass up and down the driveway, I would be spared the monster task of digging out the next day. So out I went, at one o'clock and three and again at six.

Meanwhile, emails were coming in from friends who were likewise preparing for the snow. One was planning to order pizza. Another was enjoying dinner and a movie in the comfort of pajamas.

I was shoveling.

But at some point, I found myself wondering: what if I don't shovel?

What if I don't shovel?

The implications of that question were as deep as the snow…

I emailed a friend at 6:15 p.m., my fingers still red from the cold, my hair matted down with snow: "If I don't shovel…the consequence would be? And if I don't hold up the world on my shoulders…the consequence would be?"

My answer came easily enough, this morning, when my thoughtfully-shoveled driveway was hidden beneath 24 more inches of snow. As therapist Barry Stevens reminds us: *Don't push the river (it flows by itself).*[59]

Standing in the shadow of the two-foot drift on top of my car with shovel in hand, I realized that I wasn't just trying to push a river but dredge it and realign it several feet sideways—such seemed the task of moving the snow in front of me.

And that's when the word appeared. Very clearly, as if written above me in the still-gray sky: Surrender. The thought of it washed over me and through me until I had no alternative but to put down the shovel and go inside.

Too often I push against a tide. Fight it or try to shift it. Worry about it. WORRY some more.

Shovel. SHOVEL some more.

Surrender, usually equated with white flags and giving up, was instead an opportunity for me to let go. Leave it be. Stop worrying. Drink wine.

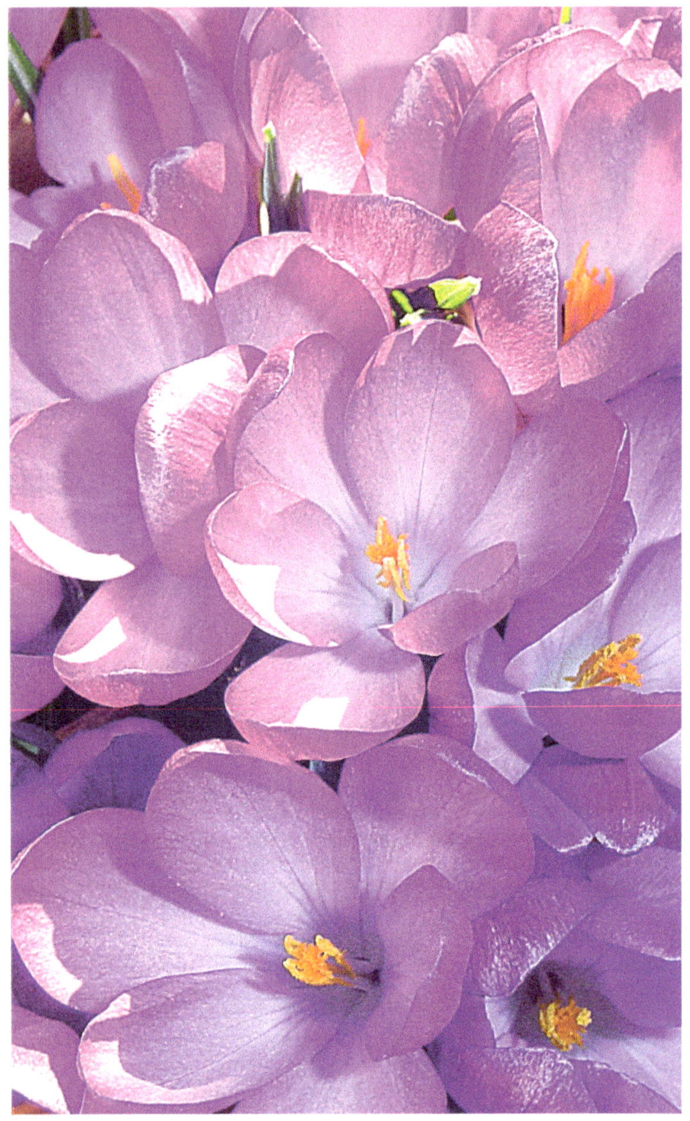

:: MARCH

Spring Arrives!

and so it springs forth

with all the potential

of sleeping bulbs

and planted seeds

with all the hope

of bated breath

and whispers of

what comes next

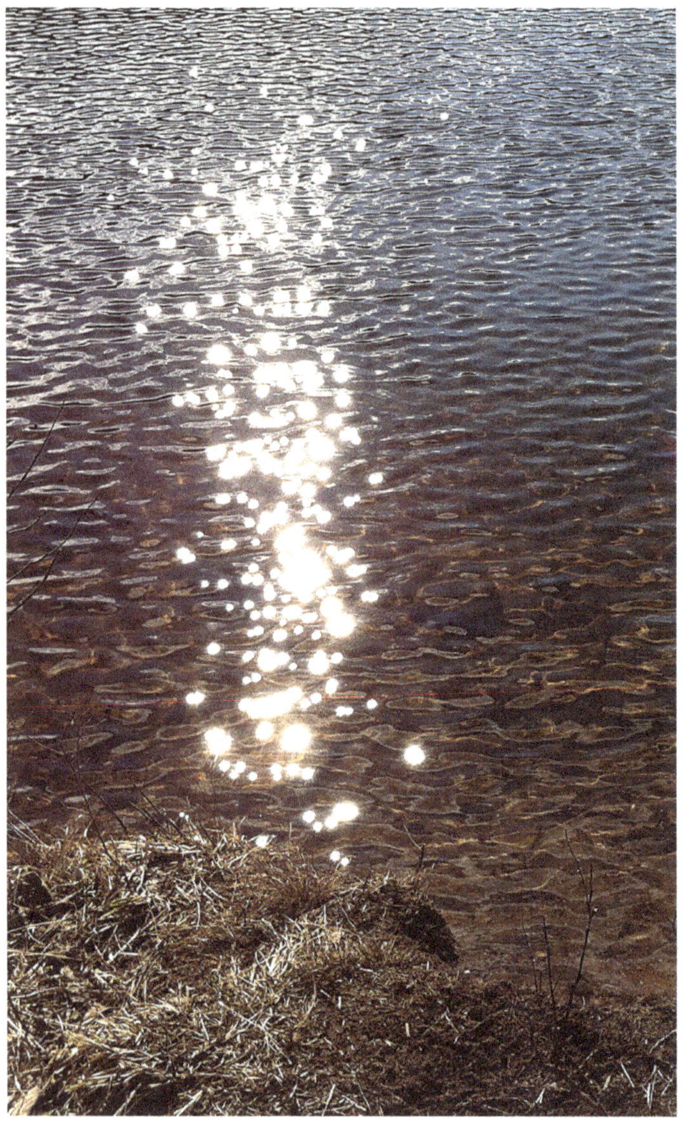

Every Moment

"Every moment is a golden one for him
who has the vision to recognize it as such."

— Fortune Cookie

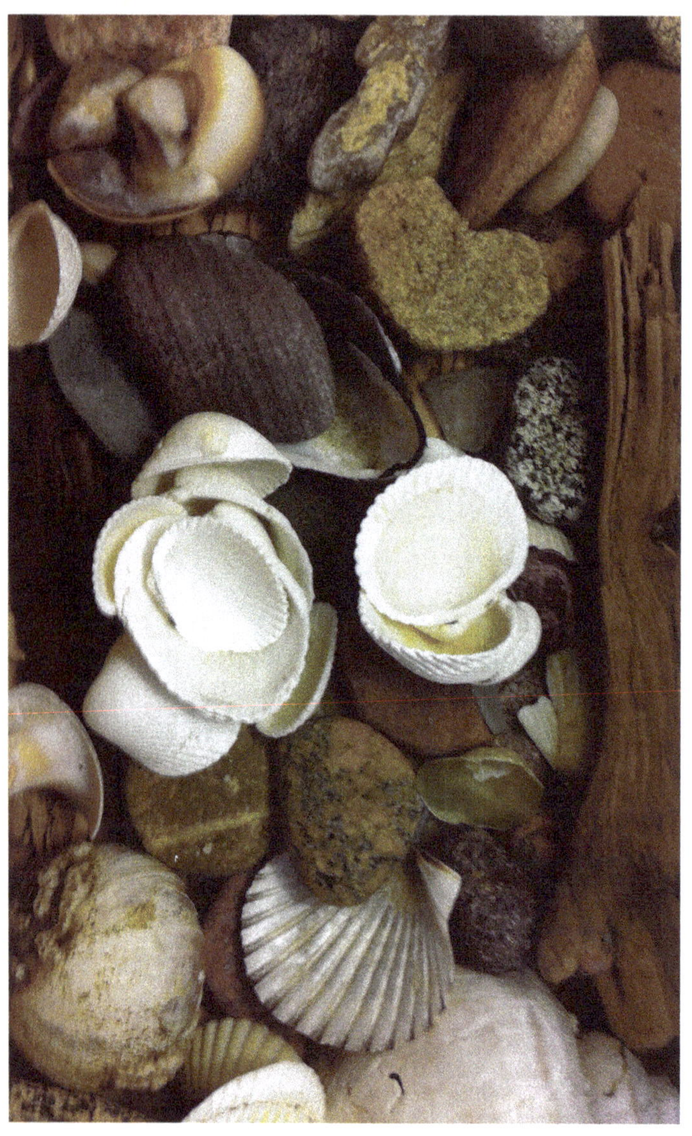

:: APRIL

Words like Abundance Are Prayer

It started simply enough: a few shells collected on the first day of vacation set down next to some small reminders to meditate.

And each day thereafter, there was more—scallop shells and sea glass, colorful stones and heart-shaped rocks, driftwood and whelk.

This small altar greeted me every morning and upon my return to the room each afternoon—a reminder of gratitude for treasures found at every step.

"What wonderful abundance," my friend Melissa commented. "I can feel the serenity."

These become the words I meditated on for the week: gratitude, abundance, serenity.

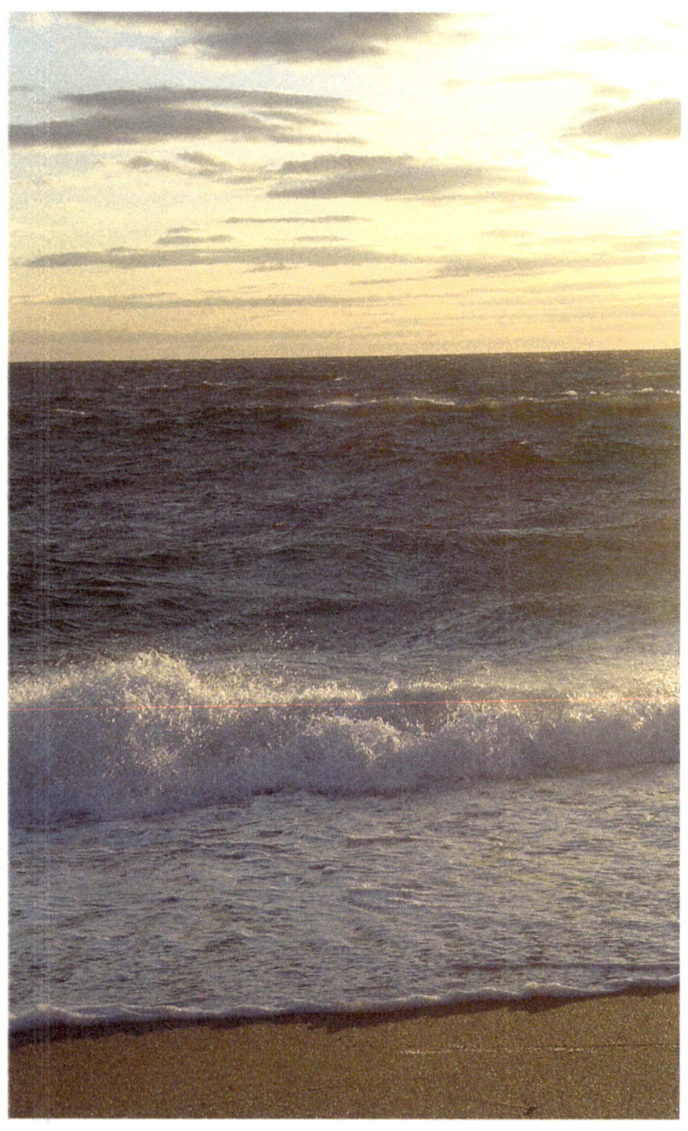

Leaving Everywhereness

There's a commercial on television for some new technology. It shows a woman visiting a grand museum but still able to access her cell phone. It rings and she answers a phone call. It rings and she sees a friend's new photos. It rings and she receives a text message.

The message is the same as the commercial showing a family on a camping trip zipped up inside their tent staring into a mobile device—why be present when you can be somewhere else?

I am just back from vacation. I called it "The Great Cape Escape," but did I really escape? It didn't matter that the hotel's Wi-Fi only worked if I was sitting with my laptop on the bathroom floor, my iPhone with its "everywhereness" allowed me instant access to everything and everyone—200 miles from home, five miles down the beach or three miles out into the ocean.

It turns out, being present—being here, in this moment—takes even more effort now than it did in 1859 when Thoreau suggested "live in the present, launch yourself on every wave, find your eternity in each moment."[60]

Because here in the 21st century, our present moment includes everyone else's present moments that are broadcast on social media and emails and blogs and websites.

Our present moment now includes these multifunctional devices that serve as our phone, camera, clock, message machine, compass, book, entertainment console, umbilical cord.

Like Medusa, it's hard to look away.

It takes mindfulness to disconnect from that everywhereness, that everythingness—you know as well as I do how it seduces us. But as we move forward, as our technology feeds our technology, we have to learn to set boundaries.

They like to say you have a right to everywhereness. But you also have a right to shut it off, to look up from the tiny little screens and see the big picture—right now, this moment. Go!

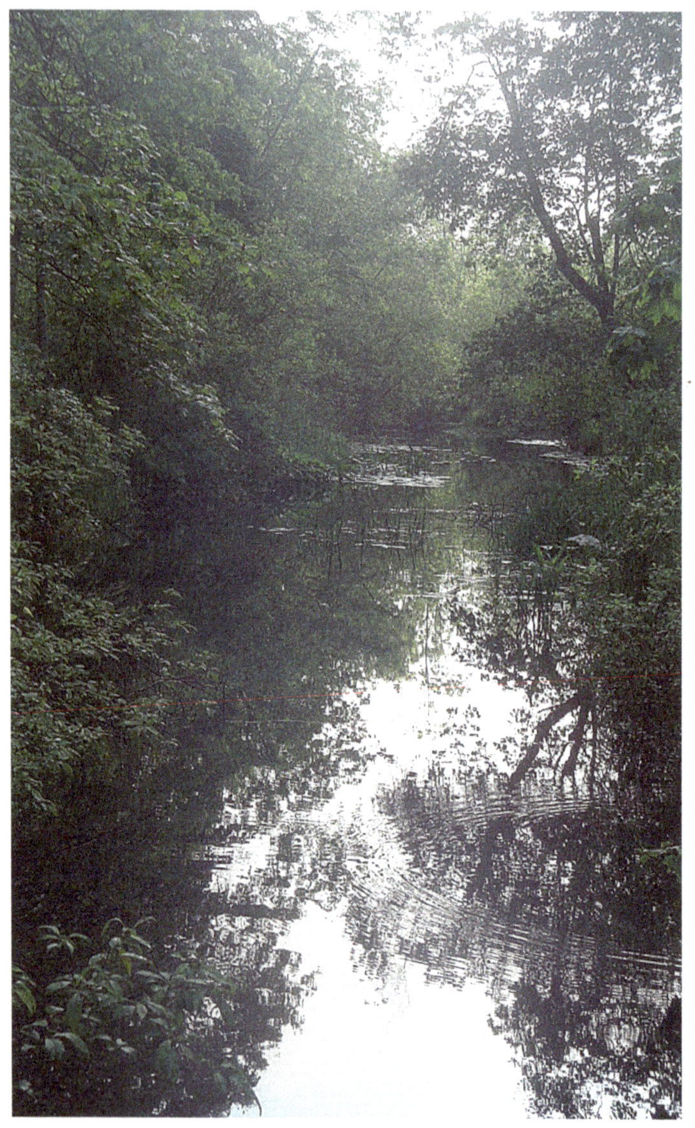

:: MAY

It's Not Everyday

By the time I made it out the door for my afternoon walk, the spring-is-here day had changed its mind. The sky overhead was an ominous dark gray, the kind that lets you know rain is on the way.

But I was not deterred and instead slipped back inside for my rain hat before heading across town to the woods.

A few parked cars were at the entrance when I arrived, no doubt belonging to the soaking wet folks jogging hurriedly towards them. How odd to be coming when they were so set on going.

I wondered about my decision as I hiked up the pock-marked trail, rain tumbling down on all sides of me. I wondered until I saw movement off to my left and noticed a red-tailed hawk watching me closely.

It's magic time in the woods when it rains...

A water-logged robin sang along with the chorus of peepers in the marsh. An osprey swooped down across the pond, silently catching supper in its talons. Raindrops glistened like jewels from branches as the sun asserted itself once again. And all around there were reminders that there is so much more to every day than our everyday.

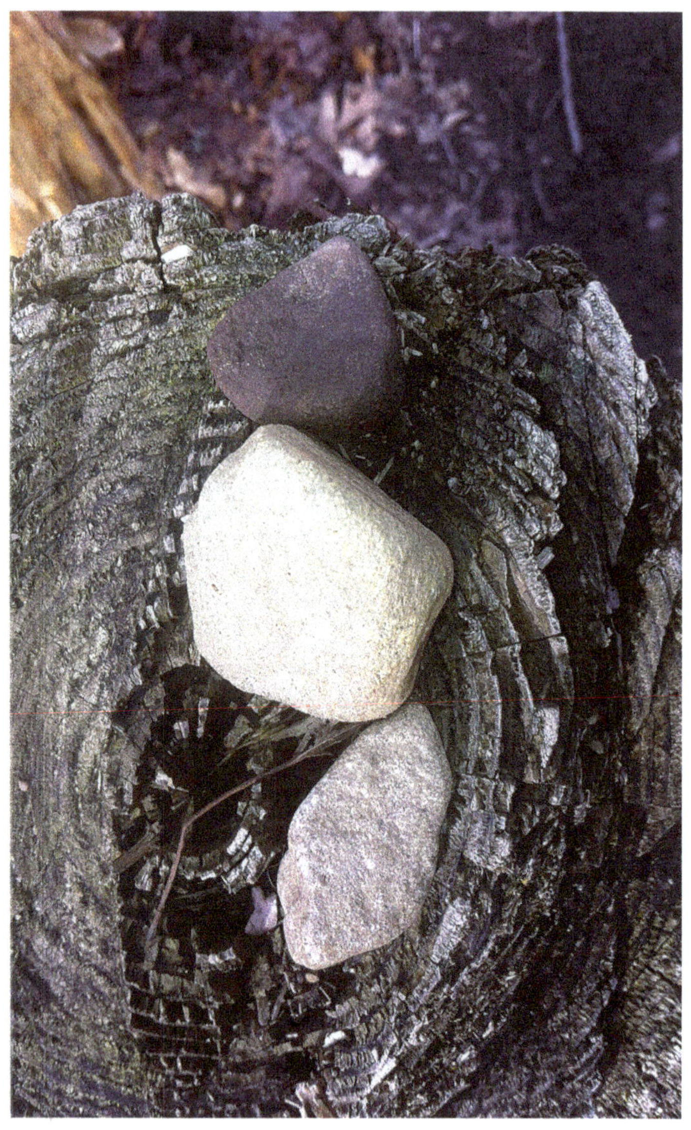

How Happy

"How happy is the little stone
That rambles in the road alone,
And doesn't care about careers,
And exigencies never fears;
Whose coat of elemental brown
A passing universe put on;
And independent as the sun,
Associates or glows alone,
Fulfilling absolute decree
In casual simplicity."

— Emily Dickinson, "Simplicity"[61]

Of Mice, Men, and Snakes

As I stepped into the woods yesterday I realized, with great disappointment, that I had forgotten my camera. Should I drive all the way back across town to retrieve it? Should I just start walking and see what happens?

The late spring heat wave that had settled in for the weekend and the bumper-to-bumper traffic on the main road were reasons enough to just get to the matter of walking. So I did.

Butterflies and dragonflies seemed suddenly all about, no doubt anticipating summer.

Bullfrogs were singing from the pond, and a turtle or two played hide-and-seek as I passed.

There were tell-tale signs of wildflowers just past their bloom, and the smell of recent rain permeated the trees.

And then, in front of me, a stunning Eastern rat snake was sunning himself in the middle of the path.

I reached for my camera, then remembered it was back at home. So the snake and I just assessed each other for a while and parted ways, he to the safety of underbrush and me to the back half of the trail—up and around the grove of pine trees, across the stream, and back to the parking lot.

I found myself remembering that you never really know what's going to happen in front of you. Whether you come prepared or not, whether you have a plan or just wing it, what comes next comes.

Maybe you get an awesome photo of a beautiful black snake. Or maybe you get the bigger picture.

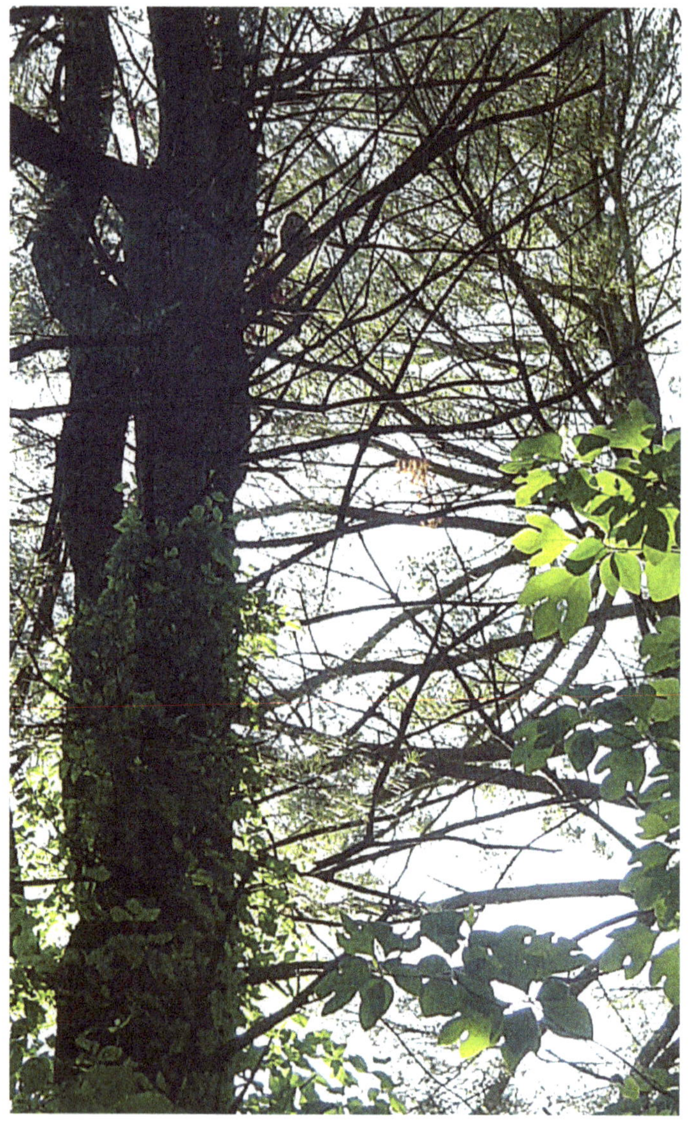

:: JUNE

A Magical Sunday

I knew it would be a magical day in the woods as soon as I turned the corner. There, near the park entrance, a baby snapping turtle was trying to cross the road. I pulled over, helped her to the other side, then made my way to the trailhead.

The sun had just found its place above the tree rise to the east, so the light in the forest was bright and bewitching, casting long shadows here, lighting trees afire there.

Two swans glided slowly near the edge of the pond, mourning, I think. The cygnet I saw two weeks ago has been absent from their side since. There seems to be a lot of that this week—mourning and finding ways to glide softly through.

At the start of the first hill, I startled two courting pileated woodpeckers. They continued down the path in front of me, ducking in and out of branches, laughing with each other. A rare and wondrous blessing!

A rustle of leaves from above caught my attention—more amorous intentions from two Cooper's hawks flirting with a display of sunlit tail feathers and song.

Nearby and seemingly unimpressed by the all the woods wooing, a barred owl sat by herself watching the spectacle. I laughed out loud when she caught me watching her watching them.

As I continued on, the trail became muddy and puddly— at one point, flooded too much to cross. It changed the sound and sense of the woods with rushing water in new places. These new places demanded new paths and direction changes, which always seems so effortless in the woods, so intrinsic.

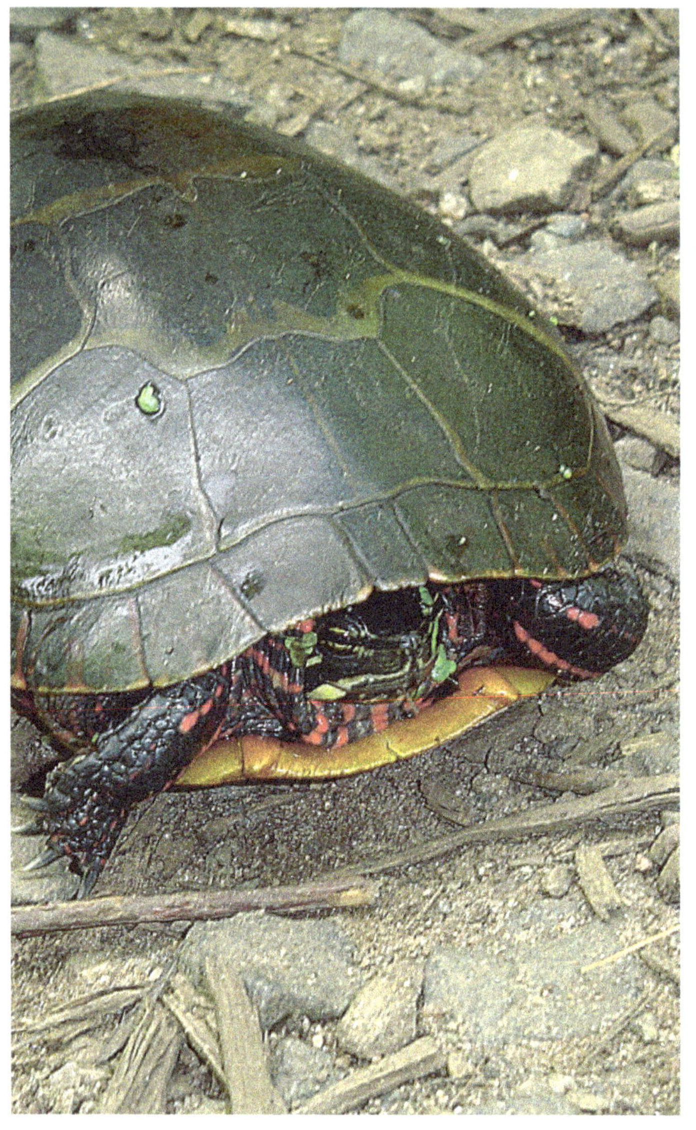

On Turtles, God, and the Intention of All This

It has certainly been an exciting time in the woods lately! Such a great abundance of animals to happen upon birds, snakes, turtles, frogs! And as I stop to take pictures and consider new writings, I find myself thinking about God.

How much closer can I get to the intention of God than to be walking in the woods and interacting—however so slightly—with these magnificent creatures? It is like Emily Dickinson observed:

> *Some keep the Sabbath going to church;*
> *I keep it staying at home,*
> *with a bobolink for a chorister,*
> *and an orchard for a dome.*[62]

EASTERN PAINTED TURTLE

Yesterday, I happened upon a red-eared slider turtle that had been hit by a car near the preserve where I walk. Its shell was broken and there was blood. Blood! I felt at once the fear and pain of this small creature and knew it was my responsibility to do something. I would no more leave an injured human on the side of the road.

Why is it, do you think, that we can drive by an animal who has been hit by a car and feel no remorse, but highways are shutdown when humans suffer similar fate?

Why is human murder a crime destined as front-page news, but animal murder is considered sport?

How can we preach, in our churches, on our Sabbaths, about kindness and love and right action, when we leave those hallowed spaces and commit atrocities to our planet and its creatures?

These are the things I wondered about as I placed the injured turtle into a cardboard box and drove it across town to the local vet.

These are the things I wondered about while I stopped traffic to let an Eastern rat snake cross the road.

These are the things I wondered about as I walked in the woods yesterday, hearing God in the sound of the rain and in the song of the birds.

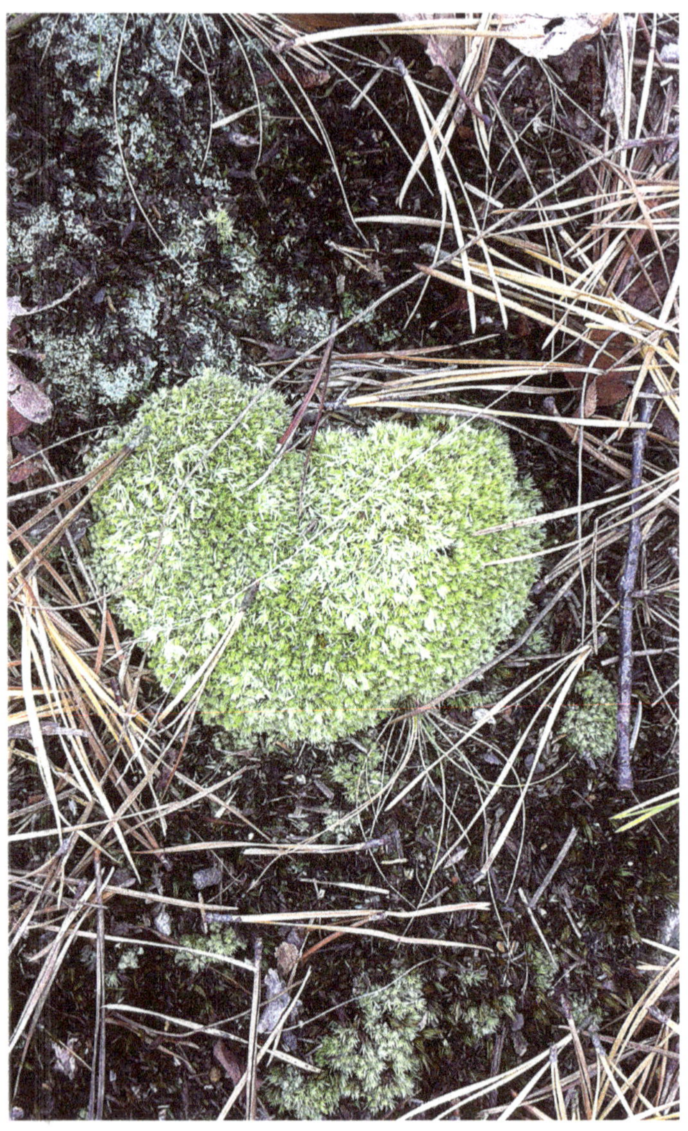

Sunday's Direction

I t was a quiet day in the woods. Overcast and cool, in the 50s with a dampness that hung in the air—leftover from the week's rains. There were no birds courting, no snakes or turtles crossing my path. Just me.

Just me and an assortment of recent conversations—with my friend Rhonda about right action and resistance, with my friend Judith about the incarnations of God, with myself about intentions and authenticity.

I took a deep breath, inhaled the smells of the pine tree and honeysuckle and whispered into the breeze—"I am asking for help, show me some direction...I'm not lost, I just don't know where I'm going."

Then I set out on my walk and almost immediately received my reply: Love.

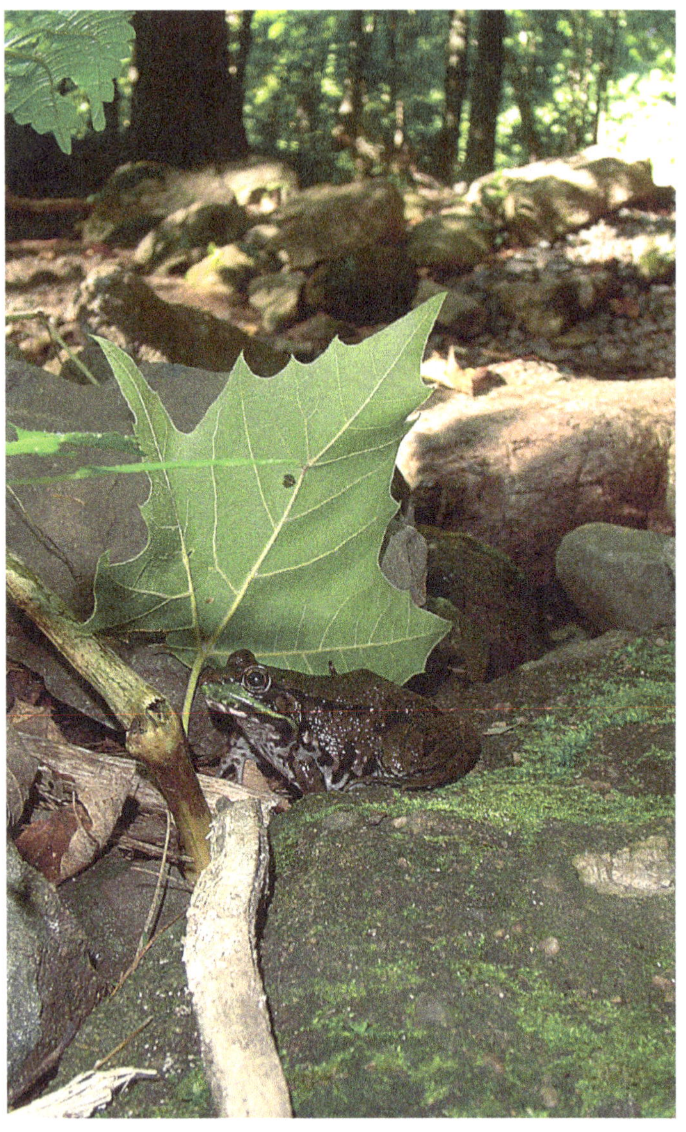

On a Frog Meditating

Teach me

how to do that

gentle soul

who sits

quietly

softly

still.

Do frogs

even have

To Do lists?

GREEN FROG

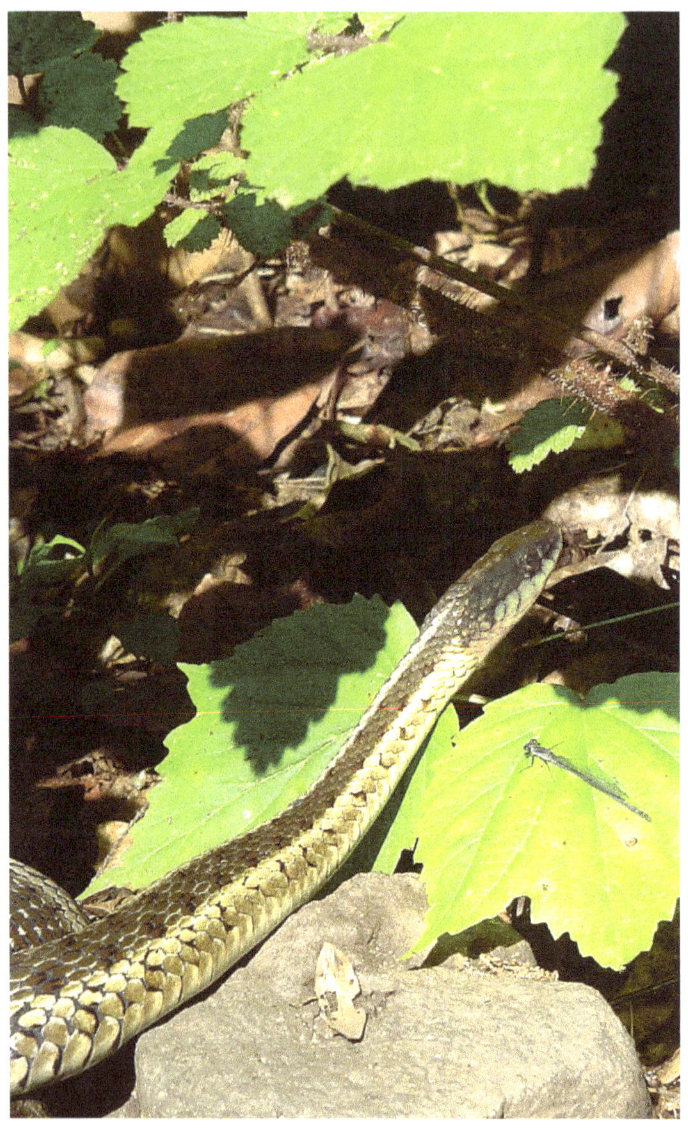

:: JULY

Charming Snakes & Kissing Frogs

In moments of stillness,

we size each other up,

I catch my breath

and hold it tightly

so as not to move.

His heart races.

I watch the pulse

that beats to

the rhythm of

my own—oneness.

COMMON GARTER SNAKE

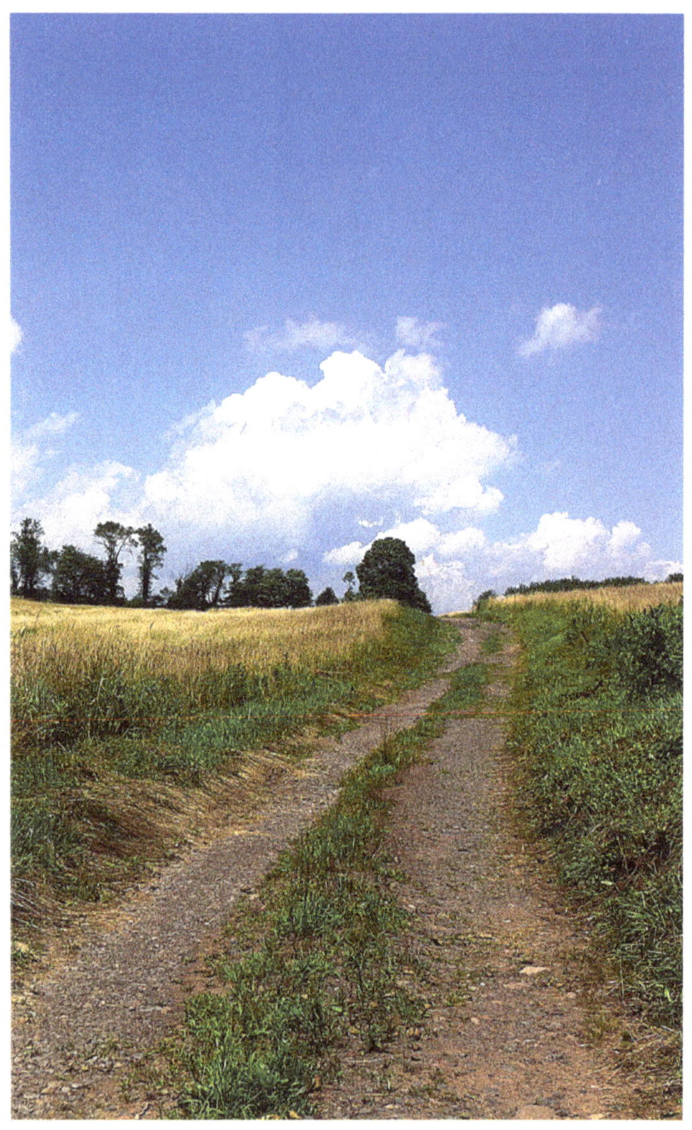

Instinctually

A phone call this week took me askew, suggesting I reconsider my direction. I was dizzy for a minute and kept walking.

A decision this week took me askew, suggesting I rethink the thinking I'd already thought. I was slowed but did not falter.

> *When I go out of the house for a walk, uncertain as yet whither I will bend my steps, and submit myself to my instinct to decide for me….*
>
> — Henry David Thoreau, "Walking"[63]

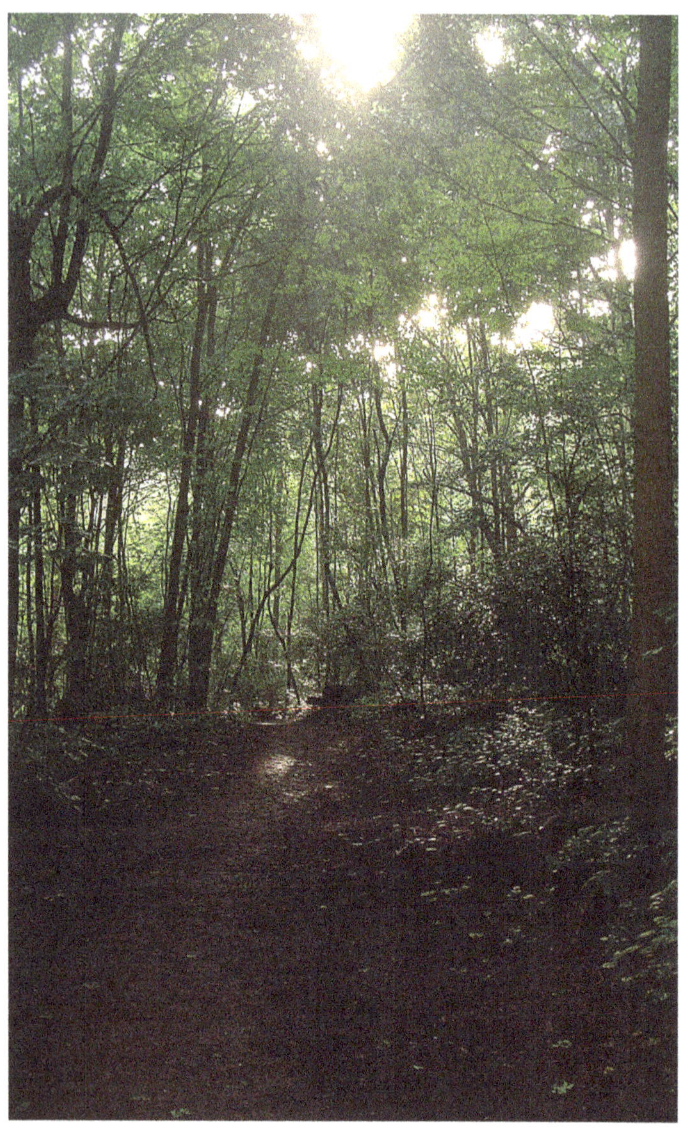

Another Way

How do I tell you
there's an easier way?
I try to lead by example—
here! over here!—
but you can't see
the forest through
the trees you've planted
around yourself.

They've grown up strong—
like you—
with roots so thick
you keep tripping over them,
thinking that is how
it's supposed to be.

But what if I told you
there's a path
where the roots go deep
and suck from the rich
and fertile Earth mother
as she holds you up safely—

would you walk that way instead?

::242

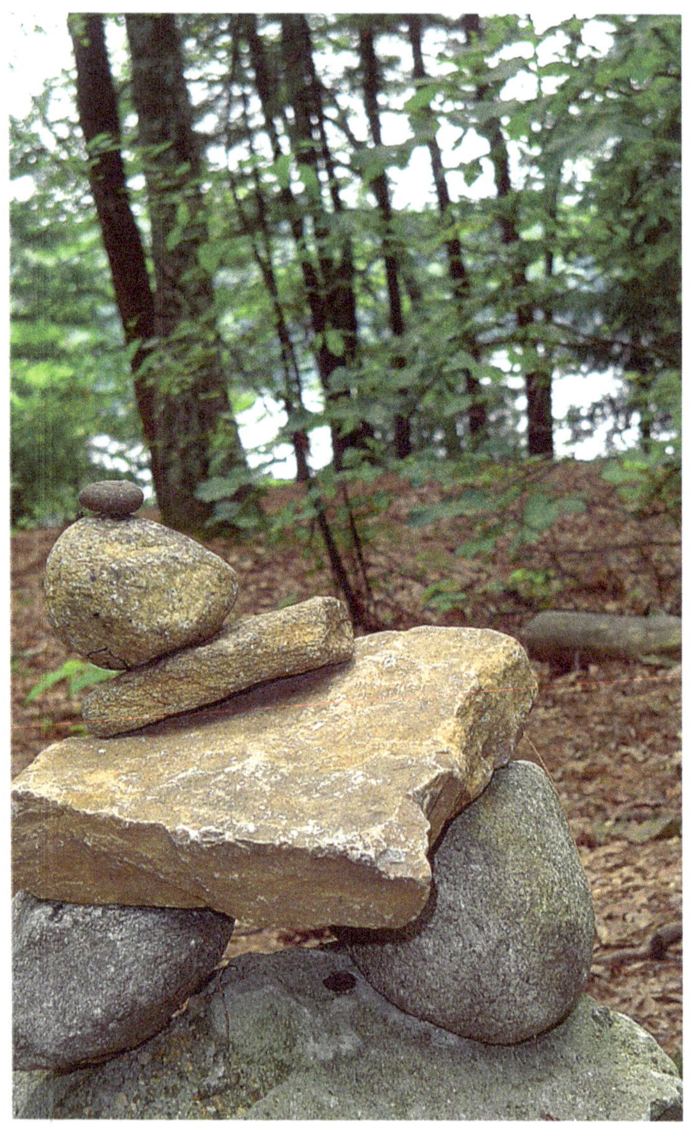

:: EPILOGUE

Just Show Up

In his classic *Walden*, Thoreau tells us: "I went to the woods because I wished to live deliberately, to front only the essential facts of life, and see if I could not learn what it had to teach...."[64] A reminder of this clear intention is carved into a wooden sign at the very spot where Thoreau built his cabin on a pond at Concord, Massachusetts in 1845.

But not everyone steps into the woods with the same clearness of purpose—I certainly did not.

When I began my practice of walking four years ago, there were no intentions at all, save for the thought that it would be good exercise (and an excuse from the gym). I never imagined what I would discover along the way!

CAIRN AT WALDEN POND

I don't know if Thoreau imagined it either, but surprisingly we found ourselves on a similar path. Each of us was called to look up from our daily life, to see Nature with open and curious eyes, to follow her lead.

And believe me, she will take the lead. Nature has a way of working herself under your skin, of becoming the song lyrics you can't get out of your head, the touchstone for another way of being in this world. She can become as familiar to you as a loved one, so that when you return again, it is as if your whole body sings "I'm home."

What I learned, what Thoreau learned—and what anyone else who begins a relationship with Nature learns—is that you don't have to go to the woods with lofty expectations. You don't have to anticipate that today will be a good walk, today I will meditate, today I will see God.

Those things just find you—like silence in prayer, like breath in yoga.

All you have to do is show up.

All you have to do is look up.

We hug the earth—how rarely we mount! Methinks we might elevate ourselves a little more. We might climb a tree, at least. I found my account in climbing a tree once. It was a tall white pine, on the top of a hill; and though I got well pitched, I was well paid for it, for I discovered new mountains in the horizon which I had never seen before,— so much more of the earth and the heavens.

— Henry David Thoreau, "Walking"[65]

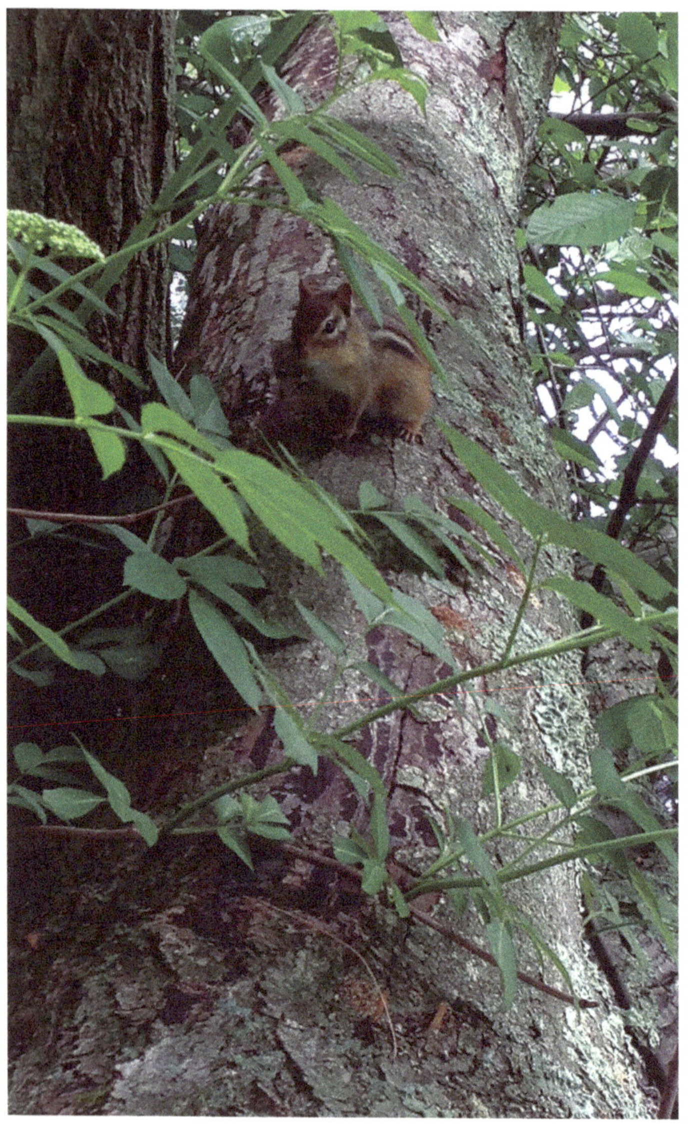

:: NOTES

ILLUSTRATIONS

pg. x   "Balance," mixed media art by Jen Payne.

pg. 104   Can you see the angel in the photo? It's fun to note that I was
           alone in the woods, this is not my shadow. When I moved, the
           apparition was still. Perhaps I was not alone after all.

*The majority of the photos in this book were taken at the Supply Ponds and the
Stony Creek Trolley Trail in Branford, Connecticut. The beach photos were taken
at the Cape Cod National Seashore in Massachusetts.*

TEXT

1   Albert W. Palmer, *The Mountain Trail and Its Message* (Boston: The
     Pilgrim Press, 1911), 27.

2   Additional essays and poems about the nature of mindfulness
     can be found on the blog *Random Acts of Writing*, http://www.
     randomactsofwriting.net.

3   Song of Solomon 2:10-12, King James Version. This version refers
     to the "voice of the turtle." Other versions use "dove," "bird," and
     "turtledove." For a discussion on this word use, see *Bible Hermeneutics*,
     published April 2012, http://hermeneutics.stackexchange.com (http://
     goo.gl/aMS8y6).

4   David K. Funkhouser, "Our Marshes Are Dying—Sea Change:
     On Connecticut's Shore, A Search For Clues To Shrinking Coastal
     Wetlands," *The Hartford Courant,* July 22, 2007.

5   Walt Whitman, "When I Heard the Learn'd Astronomer," *Leaves of
     Grass* (New York: G.P. Putnam's Sons, 1902), 32.

6   William Henry Davies, "The Best Friend," *The Collected Poems of William
     H. Davies* (New York: A. A. Knopf, 1916), 136.

7   Even more than the movie, the book *Eat, Pray, Love* (New York: Penguin Books, 2006) by Elizabeth Gilbert is filled with a number of anecdotes about the practice of meditation. It is one of the most dog-eared books on my shelf.

8   Dale Carlson, *Stop the Pain: Adult Meditations* (Branford, CT: Bick Publishing House, 2000), 74.

9   ©Johnson, Cathy, 1991. *The Naturalist's Path: Beginning the Study of Nature.* Walker Books, an imprint of Bloomsbury Publishing Inc. From the Foreword, by Ann Zwinger, page x.

10 Henry David Thoreau, "Walking." *Atlantic Monthly*, vol. 9 (1862). Project Guttenberg, revised November 2010, http://www.gutenberg. org (http://goo.gl/FHeg).

11 Commonly attributed to Ralph Waldo Emerson, this quote actually appeared in the essay *Meditations in Wall Street* by Henry Stanley Haskins (New York: William Morrow & Co., 1940). For more on this and other classic misquotes, see *The Quote Verifier: Who Said What, Where, and When*, by Ralph Keyes (New York: St. Martin's Griffin, 2006).

12 Isaac Newton's Third Law of Motion.

13 Wayne Dyer, *Staying on the Path* (Carlsbad, CA: Hay House, Inc., 2004), 325.

14 Emily Dickinson, "The Bee is not afraid of me," *Poems by Emily Dickinson*, ed. Mabel Loomis Todd and T.W. Higginson (New York: Avenel Books, 1890), 75.

15 William Shakespeare, "As You Like It," *Plays of William Shakespeare* (Boston: Charles Williams, 1813), 218.

16 Text reprinted with permission by Michael Leunig, Australian poet, cartoonist and cultural commentator. For more of his work, see http://www.leunig.com.au.

17 *The Tree of Contemplative Practices* © The Center for Contemplative Mind in Society. Northampton, MA. Concept and design by Maia Duerr; illustration by Carrie Bergman. Note: you can download a full-size copy of the *Tree of Contemplative Practices* from the website, http://www.contemplativemind.org.

18 John Muir, "The Hetch-Hetchy Valley," *Sierra Club Bulletin*, vol. VI, no. 4. (January 1908).

19 Used with permission: *Animal Speak: The Spiritual & Magical Powers of Creatures Great and Small* by Ted Andrews © 2002 Llewellyn Worldwide, Ltd. 2143 Wooddale Drive, Woodbury, MN 55125. All rights reserved. Pages 343-344.

20 Ibid, 2.

21 Hans Margolius, *Values of Life: Essays and Notes* (Miami, FL: Pandanus Press, 1971), 19. After a lengthy search that included translating a German biography, *Erinnerungen*, from the Center for Jewish History's online archives and corresponding with numerous booksellers, this often-referenced quote was finally verified with the help of Derek at Vashon Island Books (Vashon, WA), who was selling a copy of Margolius' *Values of Life* and graciously sent photos of the quote in question.

22 Barbara Upton, "The Beautiful, Mystical Owls," *Waking Planet*, accessed December 2010, http://www.wakingplanet.com/owls.html.

23 Andrews, *Animal Speak*, 153.

24 *The Dhammapada*, trans. F. Max Müller (Delhi: Motilal Banarsidass, 1965). *Project Gutenberg*, revised January 2013, http://*www.gutenberg. org (http://goo.gl/9Mhs80)*.

25 From *The Notebook* by Nicholas Sparks. Copyright ©1996 by Nicholas Sparks. By permission of Grand Central Publishing. All rights reserved. Page 182.

26 Osho, *Love, Freedom, Aloneness: The Koan of Relationships* (New York: St. Martin's Press, 2001), 216.

27 Carlson, *Stop the Pain*, 69.

28 Ibid, 69.

29 John Burroughs, "An Outlook Upon Life," *Leaf and Tendril* (Boston and New York: Houghton Mifflin Company, 1908), 261.

30 John Muir, *Steep Trails* (Boston and New York: Houghton Mifflin Company, 1918), 128.

31 Frequently attributed to either Henry David Thoreau or Nathaniel Hawthorne, this popular quote about happiness can be more directly attributed to author and social worker L. Richard Lessor. The quote appeared on popular motivational posters in the 1970s, printed by Argus Communications, and was verified by Mr. Lessor himself in a

phone call in 2014. Representatives from both the Thoreau Institute at Walden Woods and the Nathaniel Hawthorne Society were unable to identify source material for the quote.

32 Max Ehrmann, "Desiderata," 1927. Public domain text, accessed July 2011, http://en.wikipedia.org/wiki/Desiderata.

33 Judith Bruder, "Buddhas—and Ordinary People," *Touch 2 Touch*, posted on July 27, 2011, http://touch2touch.wordpress.com (http://goo.gl/db6NoY).

34 John Muir, *The Mountains of California* (New York: The Century Co., 1907), 330.

35 Andrews, *Animal Speak*, 344-347.

36 The full text of Marianne Williamson's empowering quote from *A Return to Love* is available at *Wikipedia*, accessed August 2011, http://en.wikipedia.org/wiki/Marianne_Williamson.

37 Andrews, *Animal Speak*, 344-347.

38 "Ich bin auf der Welt.../I'm too alone in the world," from *Rilke's Book of Hours: Love Poems to God* by Rainer Maria Rilke, translated by Anita Barrows and Joanna Macy, translation copyright ©1996 by Anita Barrow and Joanna Macy. Used by permission of Riverhead Books, an imprint of Penguin Group (USA) LLC. Page 67.

39 "Chapter 9," from *The Dharma Bums* by Jack Kerouac, copyright ©1958 by Jack Kerouac. Copyright renewed ©1986 by Stella Kerouac and Jan Kerouac. Used by permission of Penguin, a division of Penguin Group (USA) LLC. Pages 61-62.

40 Thoreau, *Walden*, 502.

41 Mary Oliver, "Wild Geese," *Dream Works* (New York: Atlantic Monthly Press, 1986), 14.

42 Albert W. Palmer, *The Mountain Trail and Its Message* (Boston: The Pilgrim Press, 1911), 28-29.

43 Alcoholics Anonymous, *Twelve Steps and Twelve Traditions* (New York: Alcoholic Anonymous World Services, Inc., 1952), as adapted from the original version of the "Serenity Prayer" attributed to Reinhold Niebuhr.

44 Henry David Thoreau, *Walden* (Boston and New York: Houghton Mifflin Company, 1854), 484.

45 Jon Kabat-Zinn, *Wherever You Go, There You Are: Mindfulness Meditation in Everyday Life* (New York: Hachette Book Group, Inc., 1994), 44. In this book, Kabat-Zinn quotes Thoreau extensively as example of mindful meditation—of paying attention and being more fully present in the world. Kabat-Zinn is known for his work in mind-body healing and mindfulness.

46 Excerpt from THE OUTERMOST HOUSE: A Year of Life on the Great Beach of Cape Cod by Henry Beston. Copyright © 1928, 1949, 1956 by Henry Beston. Copyright © 1977 by Elizabeth C. Beston. Reprinted by arrangement with Henry Holt and Company, LLC. All rights reserved.

47 Elizabeth Von Arnim, *The Adventures of Elizabeth in Rügen* (London: Macmillan & Co., Ltd., 1904), 7.

48 Andrews, *Animal Speak*, 340-342.

49 From *The Path to Tranquility* by Dalai Lama, edited by Renuka Singh, copyright ©1999 by the Dalai Lama and Renuka Singh. Used by permission of Viking Penguin, a division of Penguin Group (USA) LLC.

50 Robert Frost, "On a Tree Fallen Across the Road," *The Poetry of Robert Frost* (New York: Holt, Rinehart and Winston, 1969), 238.

51 ©Johnson, Cathy, 1991. *The Naturalist's Path: Beginning the Study of Nature.* Walker Books, an imprint of Bloomsbury Publishing Inc.; Introduction, page xx.

52 Kristina Goetz, "Ever mindful: Buddhist monastics practice simple life of meditation in Mississippi," *The Commercial Appeal*, published April 22, 2012, http://www.commercialappeal.com, (http://goo.gl/LQv483).

53 Elizabeth Barrett Browning, *The Complete Poetical Works of Mrs. Browning* (Boston: Houghton Mifflin Company, 1900), 372.

54 Andrews, *Animal Speak*, 172-181.

55 Ibid, 153.

56 Text from Corita, serigraph love the moment reprinted with permission from the Corita Art Center Immaculate Heart Community.

57 Andrews, *Animal Speak,* 156-157.

58 Jiddu Krishnamurti, *The Book of Life: Daily Meditations with Krishnamurti* (New York: HarperSanFrancisco, 1995), August 1 entry.

59 Taken from the title of Barry Stevens' book *Don't Push the River (It Flows by Itself)* (Lafayette, CA: Real People Press, 1970).

60 Henry David Thoreau, Franklin Benjamin Sanborn, Bradford Torrey, *The Writings of Henry David Thoreau: Journal* (Boston and New York: Houghton Mifflin Company, 1906), 159.

61 Emily Dickinson, "Simplicity," *Poems by Emily Dickinson*, Second Series, ed. T.W. Higginson and Mabel Loomis Todd (Boston: Roberts Brothers, 1891), 154.

62 Emily Dickinson, "A Service of Song," *Poems by Emily Dickinson*, 74.

63 Thoreau, "Walking," *Atlantic Monthly*, 657-674.

64 Thoreau, *Walden*, 143.

65 Thoreau, "Walking," *Atlantic Monthly*, 657-674.

* *Note: for specific, lengthy website addresses, I have used Google's URL shortener.*

** *Note: Some citations follow publishers' requested content and format.*

:: BIBLIOGRAPHY

Alcoholics Anonymous. *Twelve Steps and Twelve Traditions*. New York: Alcoholic Anonymous World Services, Inc., 1952.

Andrews, Ted. *Animal Speak: The Spiritual & Magical Powers of Creatures Great and Small*. Woodbury, MN: Llewellyn Worldwide, Ltd., 2002.

Beston, Henry. *The Outermost House: A Year of Life on the Great Beach of Cape Cod*. New York: Henry Holt and Company, 1928.

Browning, Elizabeth Barrett. *The Complete Poetical Works of Mrs. Browning*. Boston: Houghton Mifflin Company, 1900.

Bruder, Judith. "Buddhas—and Ordinary People," *Touch 2 Touch*, posted on July 27, 2011, http:touch2touch.wordpress.com/2011/07/27/buddhas-and-ordinary-people.

Burroughs, John. "An Outlook Upon Life," *Leaf and Tendril*. Boston and New York: Houghton Mifflin Company, 1908.

Carlson, Dale. *Stop the Pain: Adult Meditations*. Branford, CT: Bick Publishing House, 2000.

Carson, Rachel. *The Sense of Wonder*. New York: HarperCollins Publishers, 1956.

Davies, William Henry. "The Best Friend," *The Collected Poems of William H. Davies*. New York: A. A. Knopf, 1916.

Dickinson, Emily. *Poems by Emily Dickinson*, edited by Mabel Loomis Todd and T.W. Higginson. New York: Avenel Books, 1890.

Dickinson, Emily. *Poems by Emily Dickinson*, Second Series, edited by T.W. Higginson and Mabel Loomis Todd. Boston: Roberts Brothers, 1891.

Dyer, Wayne. *Staying on the Path*. Carlsbad, CA: Hay House, Inc., 2004.

Ehrmann, Max. "Desiderata," 1927. Public domain text, accessed July 2011, http://en.wikipedia.org/wiki/Desiderata.

Frost, Robert. "On a Tree Fallen Across the Road," *The Poetry of Robert Frost*. New York: Holt, Rinehart and Winston, 1969.

Funkhouser, David K. "Our Marshes Are Dying—Sea Change: On Connecticut's Shore, A Search For Clues To Shrinking Coastal Wetlands." *The Hartford Courant*, July 22, 2007.

Gilbert, Elizabeth. *Eat, Pray, Love*. New York: Penguin Books, 2006.

Goetz, Kristina. "Ever mindful: Buddhist monastics practice simple life of meditation in Mississippi." *The Commercial Appeal*, published April 22, 2012, http://www.commercialappeal.com, (http://goo.gl/LQv483).

Haskins, Henry Stanley. *Meditations in Wall Street*. New York: William Morrow & Co., 1940.

Johnson, Cathy. *The Naturalist's Path: Beginning the Study of Nature*. New York: Walker Books, 1991.

Kabat-Zinn, Jon. *Wherever You Go, There You Are: Mindfulness Meditation in Everyday Life*. New York: Hachette Book Group, Inc., 1994.

Kerouac, Jack. *The Dharma Bums*. New York: Penguin Books Ltd., 1958.

Krishnamurti, Jiddu. *The Book of Life: Daily Meditations with Krishnamurti*. New York: HarperSanFrancisco, 1995.

Lama, Dalai. *The Path to Tranquility*. Edited by Renuka Singh. New York: Viking Penguin, 1999.

Lindbergh, Anne Morrow. *Gift from the Sea*. New York: Vintage Books, 1978.

Margolius, Hans. *Values of Life: Essays and Notes*. Miami, FL: Pandanus Press, 1971.

Muir, John. *John of the Mountains: The Unpublished Journals of John Muir*. Edited by Linnie Marsh Wolfe. Madison, WI: University of Wisconsin Press, 1938.

Muir, John. "The Hetch-Hetchy Valley." *Sierra Club Bulletin*, vol. 6, no. 4. (January 1908).

Muir, John. *The Mountains of California*. New York: The Century Co., 1894.

Muir, John. *Steep Trails*. Boston and New York: Houghton Mifflin Company, 1918.

Oliver, Mary. *Dream Works*. New York: Atlantic Monthly Press, 1986.

Osho. *Love, Freedom, Aloneness: The Koan of Relationships*. New York: St. Martin's Press, 2001.

Palmer, Albert W. *The Mountain Trail and Its Message*. Boston: The Pilgrim Press, 1911.

Random House College Dictionary. New York: Random House, Inc., 1980.

Rilke, Rainer Maria. *Rilke's Book of Hours: Love Poems to God*. Translated by Anita Barrows and Joanna Macy. New York: Penguin Group, 1996.

Shakespeare, William. "As You Like It," *Plays of William Shakespeare*. Boston: Charles Williams, 1813.

Sparks, Nicholas. *The Notebook*. New York: Grand Central Publishing, 1996.

Stevens, Barry. *Don't Push the River (It Flows by Itself)*. Lafayette, CA: Real People Press, 1970.

The Dhammapada. Translated by F. Max Müller. Delhi: Motilal Banarsidass, 1965. Project Gutenberg, revised January 2013, http://*www.gutenberg. org (http://goo.gl/9Mhs80)*.

Thoreau, Henry David, Franklin Benjamin Sanborn, Bradford Torrey. *The Writings of Henry David Thoreau: Journal*. Boston and New York: Houghton Mifflin Company, 1906.

Thoreau, Henry David. *Walden*. Boston and New York: Houghton Mifflin Company, 1854.

Thoreau, Henry David. "Walking." *Atlantic Monthly, vol. 9* (June 1862).

Upton, Barbara. "The Beautiful, Mystical Owls." *Waking Planet*, accessed December 2010, http://www.wakingplanet.com/owls.html.

Von Arnim, Elizabeth. *The Adventures of Elizabeth in Rügen*. London: Macmillan & Co., Ltd., 1904.

Warner, Gertrude Chandler. *The Boxcar Children*. Park Ridge, IL: Albert Whitman & Company, 1942.

Whitman, Walt. "When I Heard the Learn'd Astronomer," *Leaves of Grass*. New York: G.P. Putnam's Sons, 1902.

Williamson, Marianne. *A Return to Love*. New York: HarperCollins Publishers, 1992.

:: INDEX OF TITLES

:: INDEX OF QUOTES

:: ABOUT THE AUTHOR

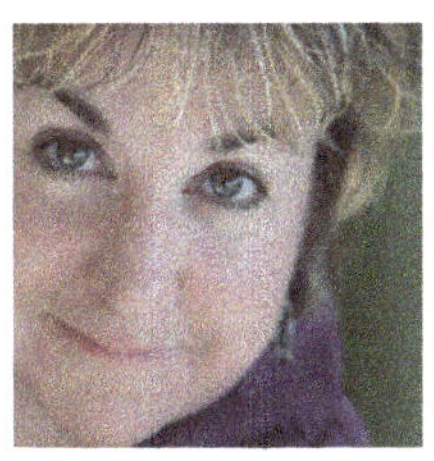

JEN PAYNE is inspired by those life moments that move us most — love and loss, joy and disappointment, milestones and turning points. When she is not exploring our connections with one another, she enjoys contemplating our relationships with nature, creativity, and spirituality. Ultimately, she believes it is the alchemy of those things that helps us find balance in this frenetic, spinning world.

Her work has also been featured in numerous publications and anthologies. In addition to *Look Up!*, Jen has published four books: *Evidence of Flossing: What We Leave Behind*, *Waiting Out the Storm*, *Water Under The Bridge: A Sort-of Love Story*, and *Sleeping with Ghosts*.

She is the owners of Words by Jen and Three Chairs Publishing, based in Branford, Connecticut, and she writes regularly at Random Acts of Writing.

Go to linktr.ee/jenpayne or click on the QR code below to see a complete list of her website and social media links.

www.ingramcontent.com/pod-product-compliance
Lightning Source LLC
Chambersburg PA
CBHW050024040726

47599CB00015B/1522